An o

CYCLE LONDON

Written by
RACHEL SEGAL HAMILTON

Other opinionated guides:

East London *Big Kids' London*
London Architecture *Art London*
Vegan London *Free London*
London Green Spaces *Queer London*
Independent London *London Delis*
London Pubs *London Hotels*
Sweet London *Historic London*
Kids' London *Margate*
Escape London *Brighton*
Eco London

INFORMATION IS DEAD.
LONG LIVE OPINION.

I've cycled in London all my life. It's not only the best way across town, it's also (by a considerable margin) the fastest. More and more people are beginning to realise that bikes suit this city better than cars, just as we now realise that bikes suit the planet better than cars. Slowly but surely, London is getting safer and greener, and so it's easier than ever to explore the capital on two wheels.

The purpose of these guides is not to tell you everything you could possibly know. Anyone can use Google. We want to cut out the noise and tell you just what you need to know. So here it is: a pithy, stripped-back, single-speed, steel racing guidebook. Hop on and enjoy the ride.

Martin, co-founder of Hoxton Mini Press

Opposite: Temple Cycles (no.10)

Richmond Park (Ride 3)
Opposite: Victoria Embankment (Ride 1)

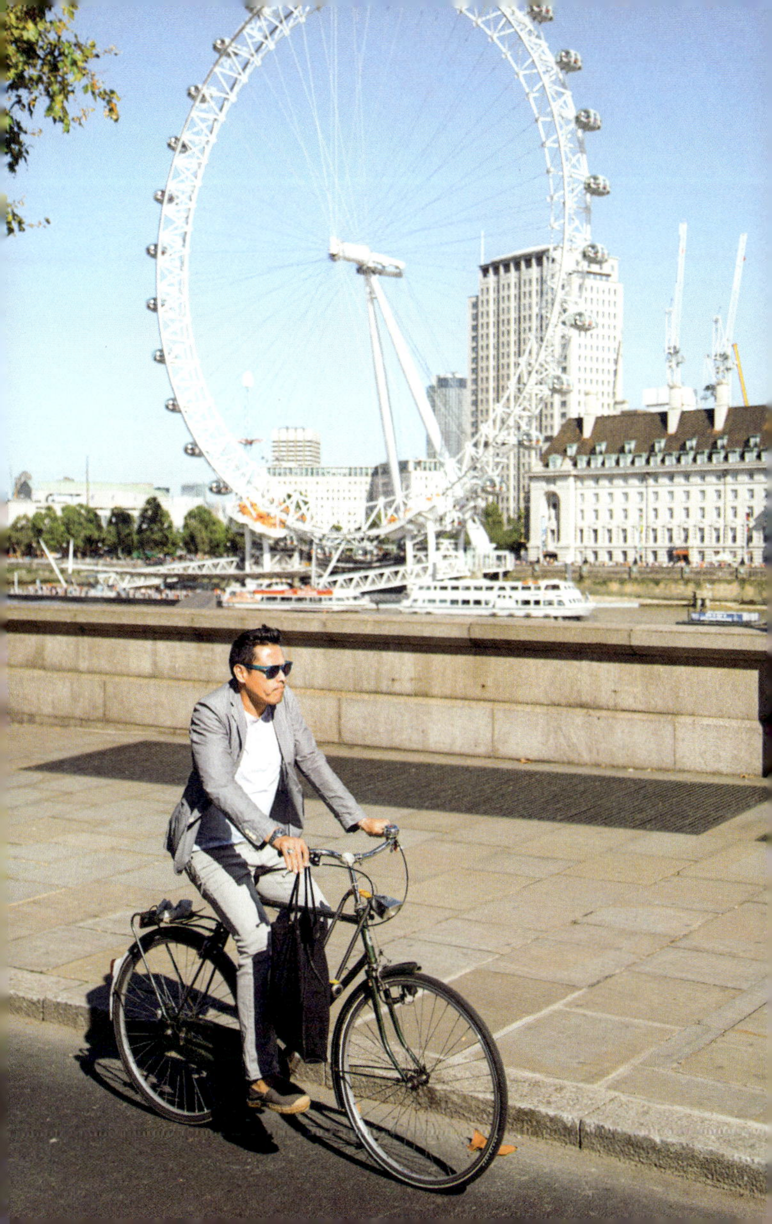

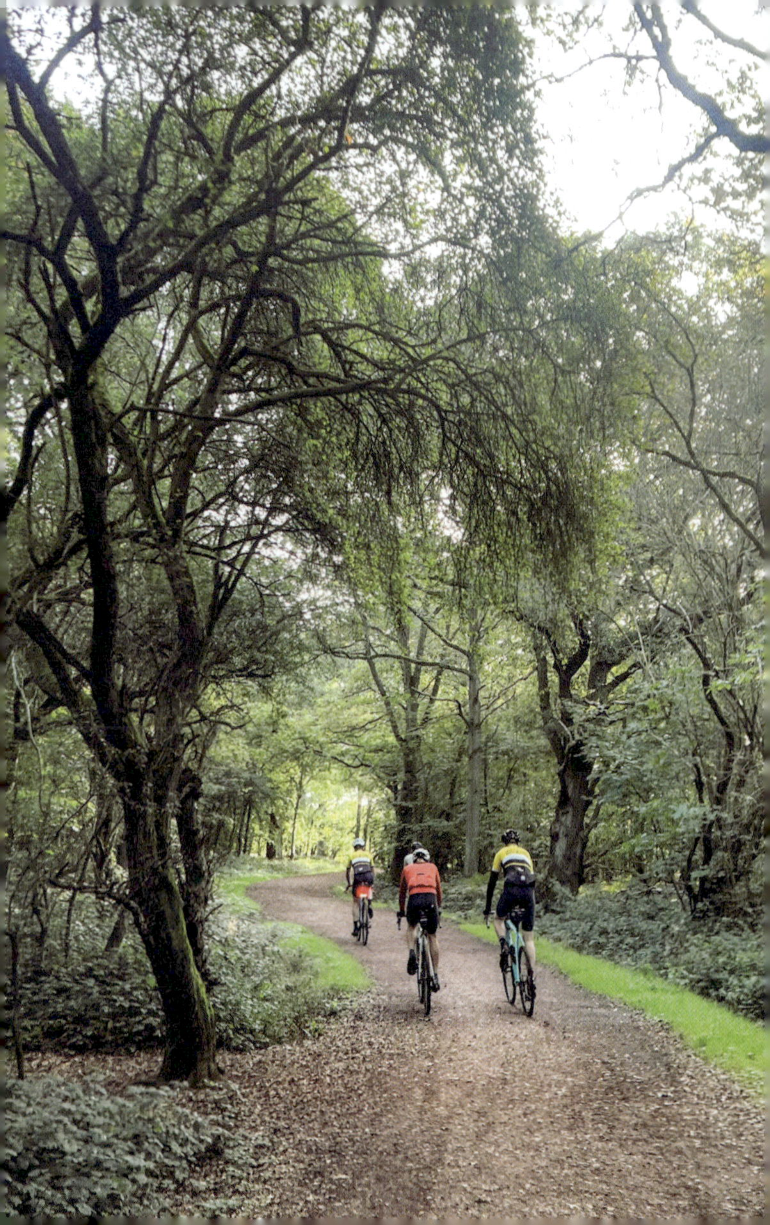

VIA Atelier (no.32)
Opposite: *Epping Forest (Ride 7)*

WHY WOULD ANYONE CYCLE IN LONDON?

In the past 20 years, cycling in the capital has changed beyond recognition. The streets of London are now paved with bike lanes – 210 glorious miles of them and counting. With the introduction of the Congestion Charge in 2003 and the Ultra Low Emission Zone in 2019, driving in the city has become less appealing, alongside which there has been a concerted effort to make cycling attractive to everyone. Spurred on by the likes of the London Cycling Campaign (no.5), Transport for London (TfL) has rolled out a network of speedy 'cycleways' (pages 14-15), connecting usually rivalrous territories of north, south, east and west through protected bike lanes, filtered side streets, canal towpaths, parks and cycle priority junctions, with more planned.

It's a far cry from when I started cycling to work regularly more than a decade ago. I'd bought a £50 bike on a whim at a second-hand shop called Cycooldelic with a resident pet lizard (only in London), but it took me weeks of intensive route-planning before I finally joined the two-wheeled rush-hour throng. Cycling in London then was daunting, a niche pursuit for daredevils – but now it's hard to think of a reason *not* to get on your bike.

Today, you'll see all sorts of Londoners pulling up at the lights. Alongside the MAMILs (for the uninitiated, that's middle-aged men in Lycra) are delivery riders on e-cargo trikes, parents on longtails picked up at London Green Cycles (no.34) and out-of-towners on rentals looking slightly lost. TfL launched its bike hire scheme in 2010, three years after Paris led the way with Vélib' Métropole. A record-breaking 11,506,889 journeys were made in 2022 using the Santander-sponsored step-throughs, which you'll see – together with competitors Lime, HumanForest and (our personal favourites) Brompton (no.6) – gleefully sailing past traffic (or abandoned on pavements).

Many of London's newest cyclists found their wheels during the pandemic. Bike shops saw an explosion in sales. Sure, some lockdown purchases ended up on eBay, but that boom took us closer to mass cycling, accelerating London's bike infrastructure and reimagining the cityscape. We should be proud of our thriving scene – the iconic community venues such as Herne Hill Velodrome (no.20); social projects that use cycling as a force for good, supporting refugees (no.17) or getting prison leavers back into work (no.23); and the London-based bike-makers, such as Stayer (no.9) and Quirk (no.15), pedal-powering a craft revolution from their workshops.

Before the 1950s, cycling was a default mode of transport for London, until cars took over; with the climate emergency rapidly reshaping everything we do, this is coming full circle. Cycling isn't just better for the environment; it's better for our well-being. Don't believe everything you hear about a supposed 'culture war' raging between cyclists and motorists; this is a battle that's already been won.

Rachel Segal Hamilton, 2023

SEASONAL EVENTS

CRITICAL MASS LONDON

This monthly leaderless ride began in 1990s San Francisco and now takes place in cities across the world. Motivated by the theory of safety in numbers, Critical Mass is bike activism in action, temporarily taking over roads usually dominated by cars. A utopian taste of what a cycling city would feel like.

Last Friday of every month, 6pm, under Waterloo Bridge on the South Bank / see Critical Mass London on Facebook

KIDICAL MASS LONDON

This offspring of the Critical Mass movement is all about the next generation. There's nothing quite like seeing hordes of smiling kids propelling themselves along or in child seats powered by grown-ups on cargo bikes, tandems or tagalongs. Rides are organised ad hoc by local parents in neighbourhoods across the capital.

Various dates / see Kidical Mass UK on Facebook

THE CYCLE SHOW

Alexandra Palace is transformed into the place to be for all things cycling. The biggest industry event of its kind in the country, this annual fair provides ample opportunities to geek out over cutting-edge kit from hundreds of big brands and smaller makers. Watch demos, test-ride bikes or listen to inspiring talks from the who's who of the two-wheeled world.

April / cycleshow.co.uk

FORD RIDELONDON

There's something for everyone at this springtime ride around London and neighbouring Essex. Take your pick from 100-mile, 60-mile or 30-mile rides, or just a free cycle through town. Essentially the London Marathon on wheels.

May / ridelondon.co.uk

DUNWICH DYNAMO

If there's one event to tick off your bucket list, let it be this. A night-time ride heading out of east London that ends on the Suffolk coast as the sun rises. Atmospheric, exhausting, exhilarating and worth every minute of missed sleep.

July / dunwichdynamo.co.uk

BLACK UNITY BIKE RIDE

Cycling has an image problem. The stereotype of the MAMIL doesn't reflect the diversity of Londoners on bikes. This annual ride from the north to the south of the city sets out to change that, inviting the capital's Black communities to celebrate their love of cycling and inspire others to join.

August / blackunitybikeride.com

DRUM & BASS ON THE BIKE

Unable to put on parties during lockdown, DJ Dom Whiting picked up a cargo trike on eBay, strapped on his decks and took to the streets, blasting out tunes. He soon attracted crowds and has since taken his cult DnB bike rides to cities across the UK.

Various dates / see @domwhiting on Twitter

CENTRAL LONDON CYCLE LANES

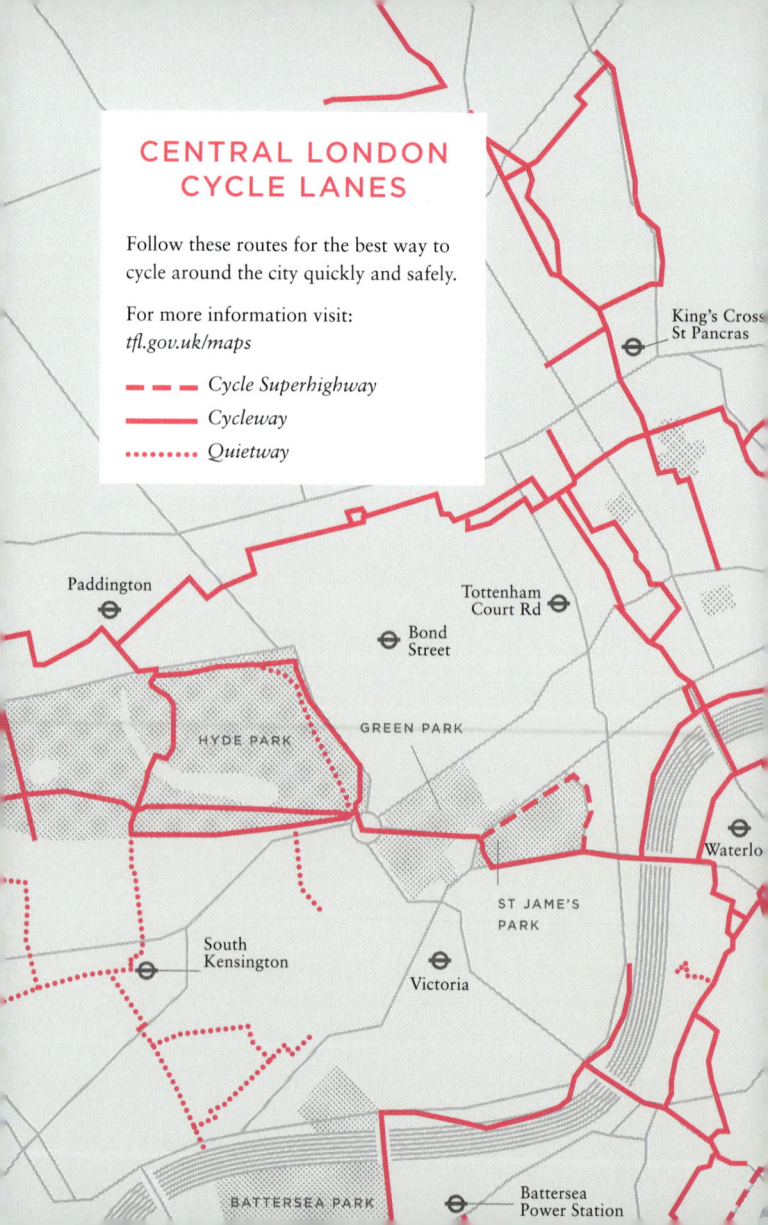

Follow these routes for the best way to cycle around the city quickly and safely.

For more information visit:
tfl.gov.uk/maps

— — — *Cycle Superhighway*
——— *Cycleway*
······· *Quietway*

Dalston Junction

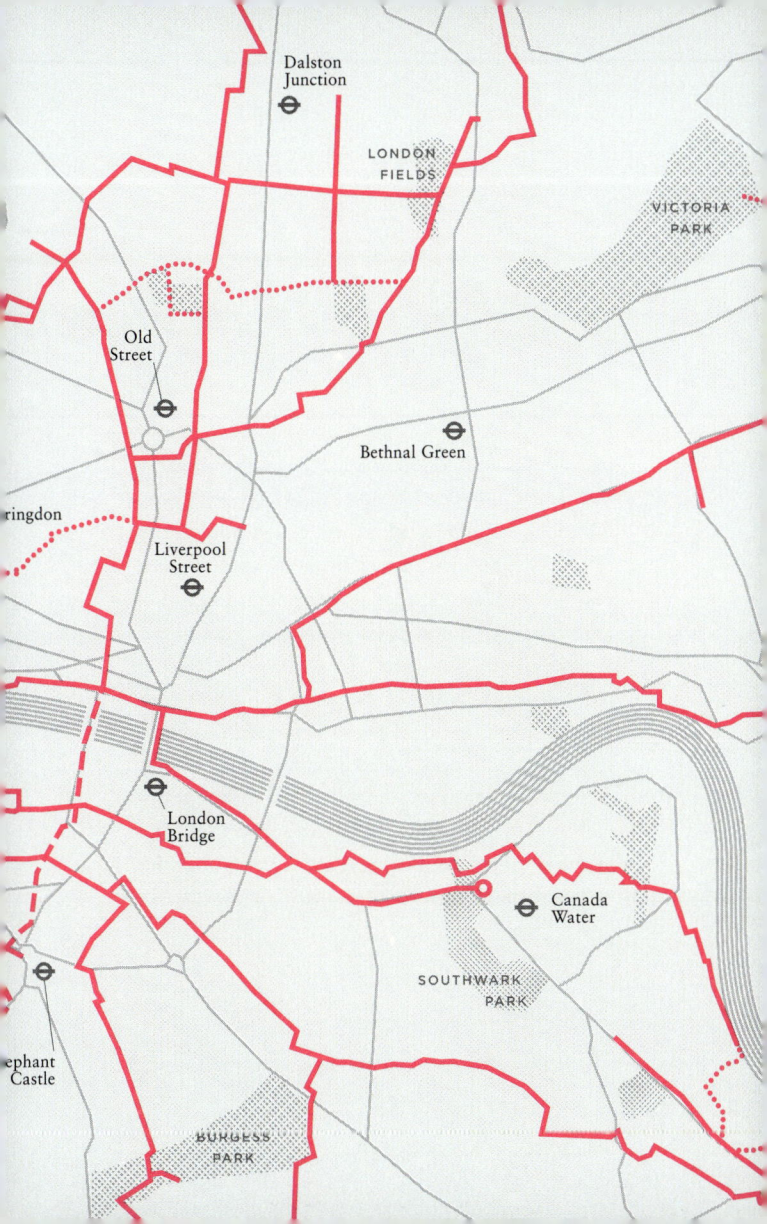

LONDON FIELDS

VICTORIA PARK

Old Street

Bethnal Green

ringdon

Liverpool Street

London Bridge

Canada Water

SOUTHWARK PARK

ephant Castle

BURGESS PARK

CENTRAL

1
CONDOR CYCLES

Legendary homegrown store

It's hard to think of a more quintessentially British bike brand than Condor. Since 1948, the shop has seen generations of London cyclists come through its doors, including celebrated cyclist and winner of the Giro (Italy's answer to the Tour de France) Tao Geoghegan Hart, who once had a weekend job here. Over three levels you'll find pretty much anything you could need. In the basement showroom you can drop off your bike for a service or pick up a new one designed in-house with a custom spec. Keep your eyes peeled and you'll spot Condor bikes all over the capital, from sleek, contemporary carbon frames to characterful vintage models. That seamless blend of heritage and cutting-edge has rightly earned Condor cult status.

49–53 Gray's Inn Road, WC1X 8PP
Nearest stations: Chancery Lane, Russell Square
condorcycles.com

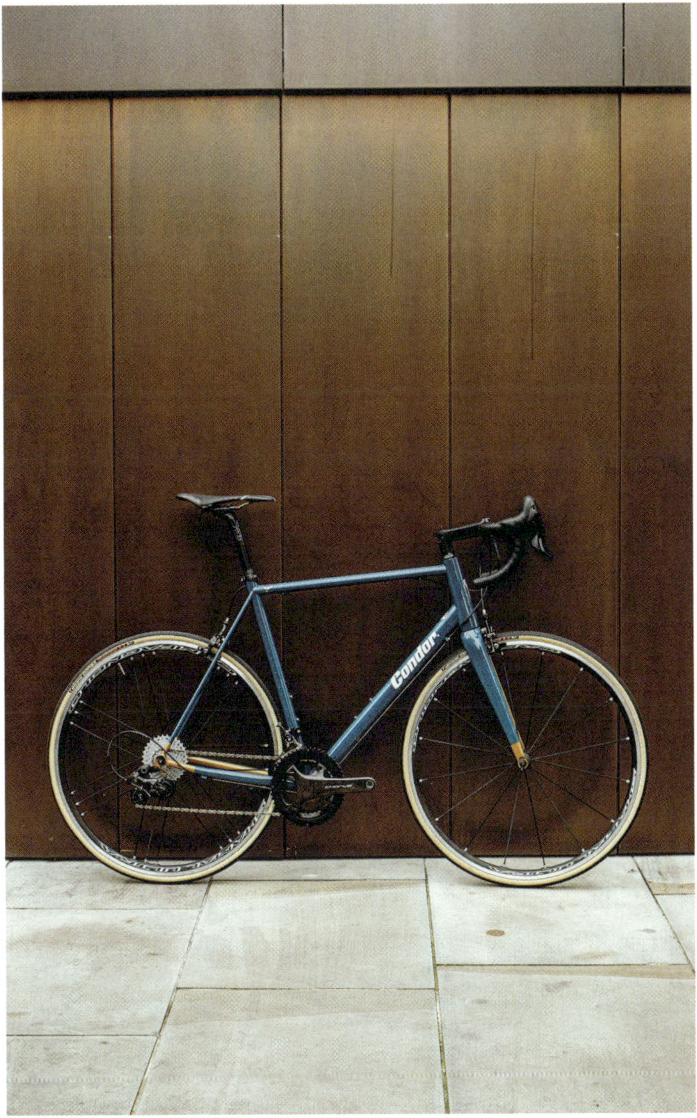
Condor.

PERFORMANCE ROAD

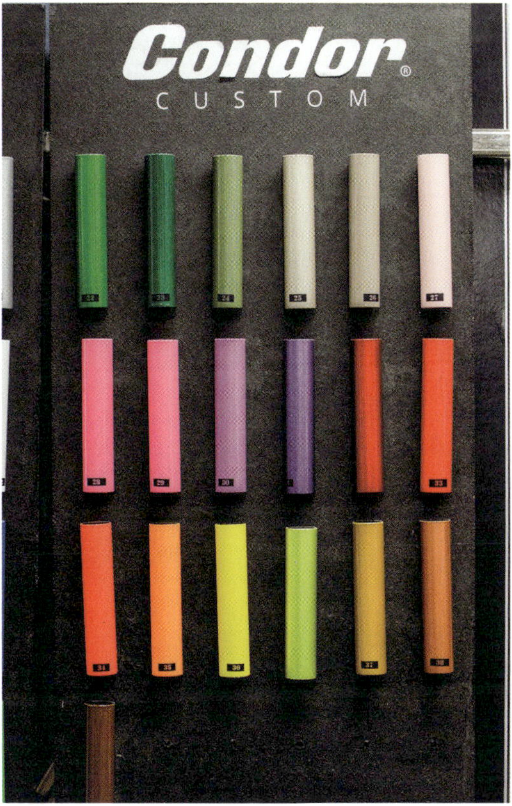
Condor®
CUSTOM

CENTRAL

2

TOKYOBIKE

A slice of Japan in Shoreditch

Riding a bike isn't always about speed. Sometimes it's quite the opposite – a way of slowing down, soaking up your surroundings, appreciating the sights, sounds and smells of the city. That's the ethos behind tokyobike. The shop is an oasis of minimalism in the heart of the East End, all white walls, wooden floors and bikes neatly lined up in rows. Simple in design, these lightweight, slim-framed steel bicycles were conceived in 2002 as a relaxed alternative to the road bike or the 'mamacharis' that fill the streets of Tokyo. They're available in an array of tasteful colours, built to last a lifetime (and priced accordingly) – and Londoners can't get enough of them.

87–89 Tabernacle Street, EC2A 4BA
Nearest station: Old Street
tokyobike.co.uk

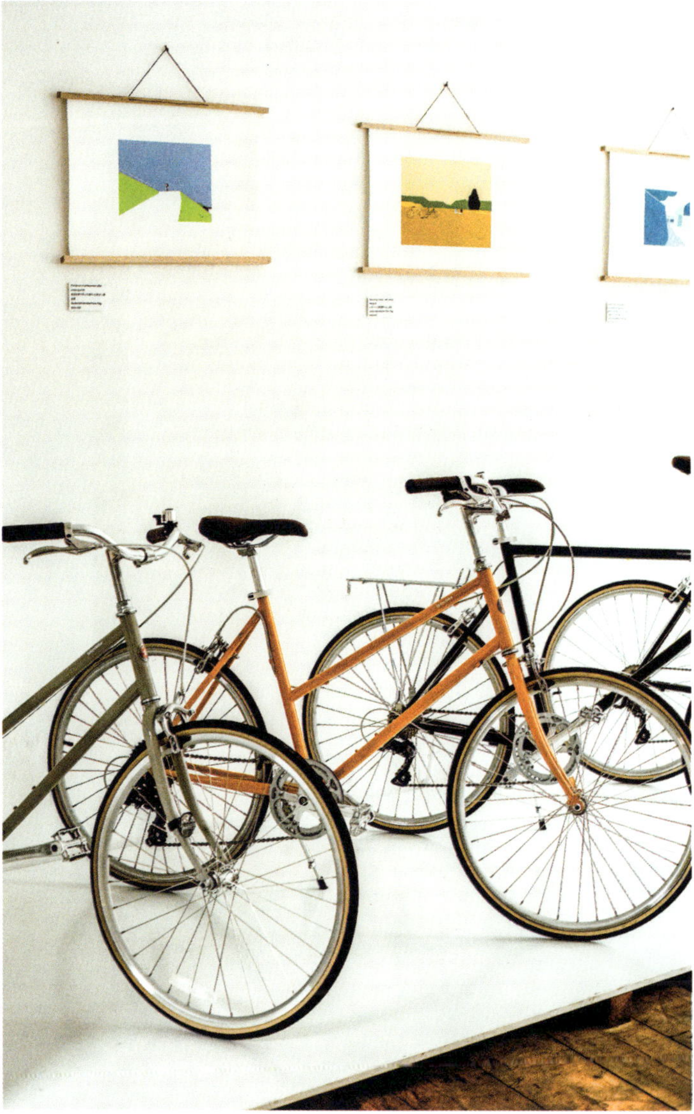

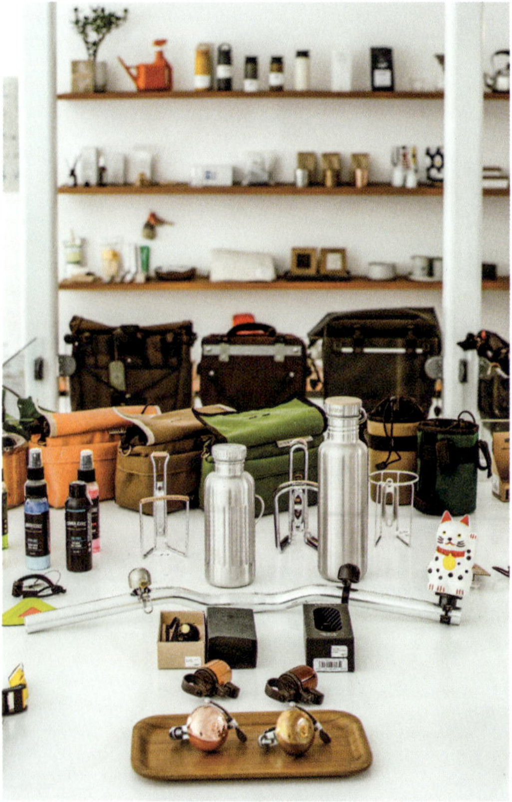

ひらがな表
わ ら や ま は な た さ か あ
り み ひ に ち し き い
を る ゆ む ふ ぬ つ す く う
れ め へ ね て せ け え
ん ろ よ も ほ の と そ こ お
LOST
LANES
NORTH

3
CYCLEFIT

Get an expert bike fitting

As easy as riding a bike, or so the saying goes. But the truth is there is a complex science to the way our bodies fit our bikes. The human form is nuanced and imperfect. Bikes are rigid structures originally designed in the Victorian era. The precise degree to which your leg extends as you pedal, the flexibility of your hips, the position of your feet: these subtle variants can be the difference between winning the race and coming a sorrowful second. They can also be the difference between hanging up your clip-ins on retirement and keeping on cycling well into your golden years. CycleFit's team of physios, podiatrists and osteopaths can provide a full bike and body MOT. Custom bikes designed in-house are available to buy, too.

The Fire Station, 14 West Central Street, WC1A 1JH
Nearest stations: Holborn, Tottenham Court Road
Other location: Bloomsbury
cyclefit.co.uk

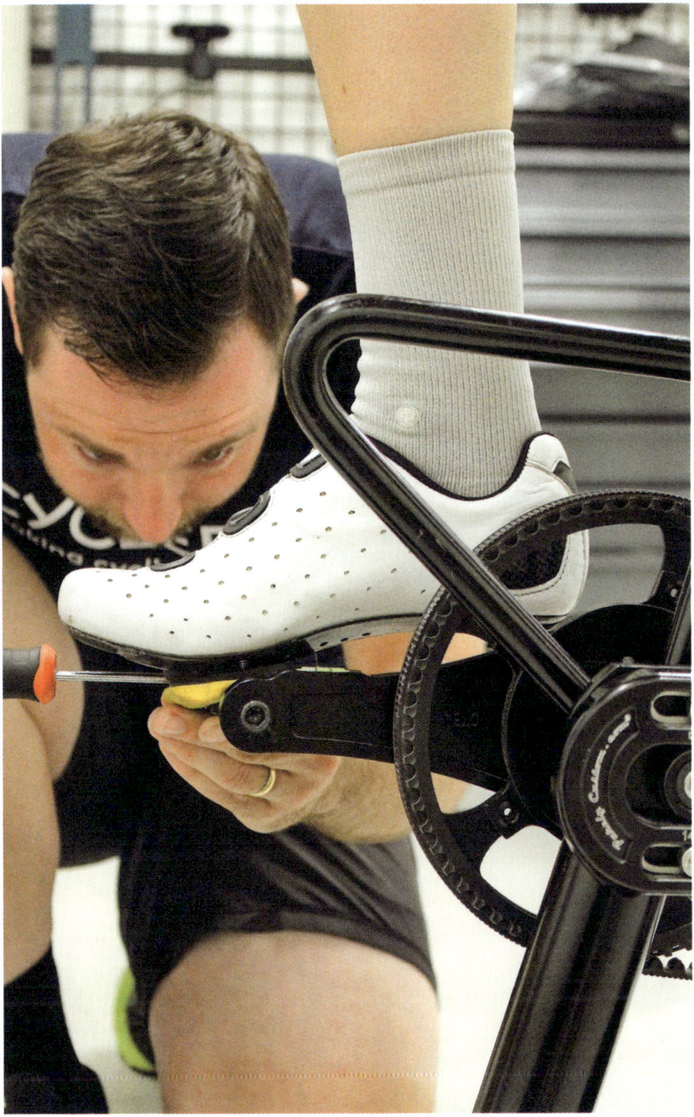

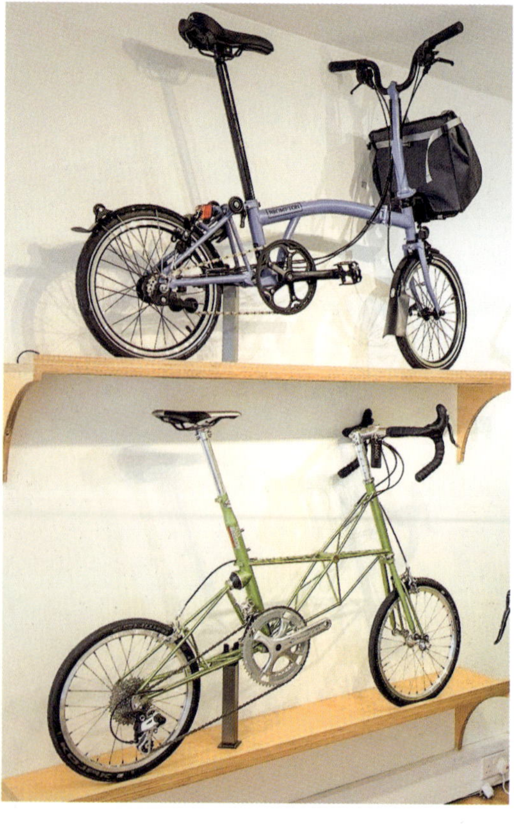

3
CYCLEFIT Store St.
CYCLEFIT
making cycling better
Bicycles
Workshop
Bike Rental
Bike Fitting
www.cyclefit.co.uk

4
PEDAL ME

Taxi and delivery services by cargo bike

How should a bike-loving bride or groom arrive at their wedding? On two wheels of course. With their hot pink branded Urban Arrows, Pedal Me is a new breed of delivery service by electric cargo bike, operating within a nine-mile radius of London. And it's not just happy couples they cart around the city. You can book them as a taxi service or as a low-carbon, niftier alternative to a removals van. Hit up their Instagram and marvel at some of the implausibly proportioned loads they manage to transport around the city, seemingly without breaking a sweat.

pedalme.co.uk

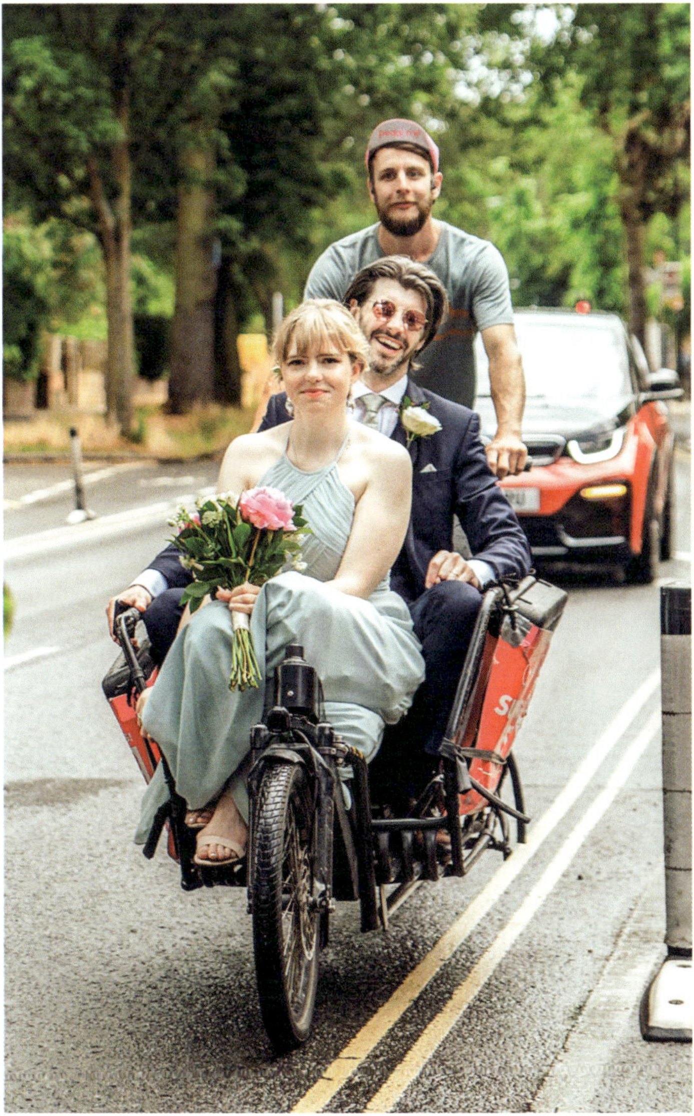

CENTRAL

5

LONDON CYCLING CAMPAIGN

A force for change

Today our roads are brimming with cyclists. There are more than 1.2 million daily trips by bike in London, many of them through our enviable new protected bike lanes and low traffic neighbourhoods. You have these folks to thank. LCC's 'Love London, Go Dutch' campaign, which kicked off in 2012, was a catalyst for reimagining our urban infrastructure, giving London cycling mass appeal. Sure, we're not quite on a par with Copenhagen yet, but we're pedalling in the right direction. Membership comes with many perks: free third-party liability insurance, discounts, legal advice and, best of all, a warm fuzzy feeling that you're changing London for the better.

Unit 206, The Record Hall,
16–16A Baldwin's Gardens, EC1N 7RJ
(By appointment only)
Nearest station: Chancery Lane
lcc.org.uk

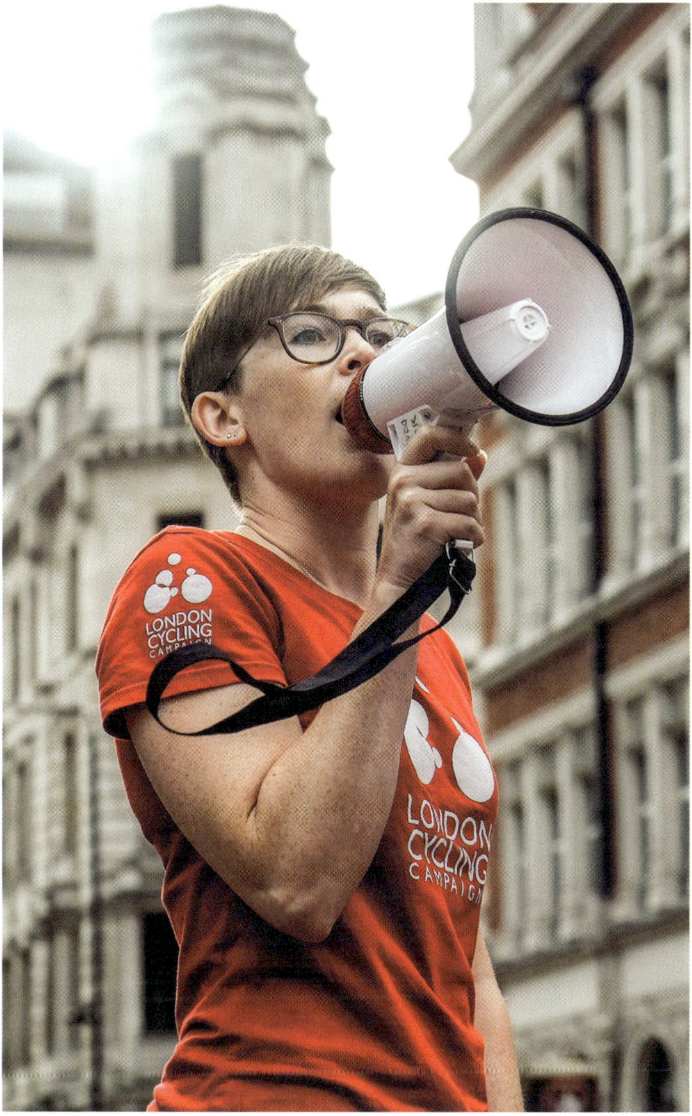
LONDON
CYCLING
CAMPAIGN
LONDON
CYCLING
CAMPAIGN

6
BROMPTON BIKE HIRE

Hire a British icon

At the time of writing there are at least five different companies operating app-based bike rental schemes across London – from eye-popping green-fronted Lime bikes to old-school scarlet Santanders (the fleet formerly known as 'Boris bikes', although they were Ken's idea originally) – each with its own varied rules and costs, which can end up getting pretty expensive. You may feel bewildered at the prospect of deciding which to go for, so we'll make it easy for you: hire a Brompton! It will cost you a mere £5 for 24 hours. If you need to jump on a tube or in a cab, you simply fold it and go. Plus, it's a design classic. Just drop it off at one of their 38 docks when you're done.

Docks in various locations, see website for details
bromptonhire.com

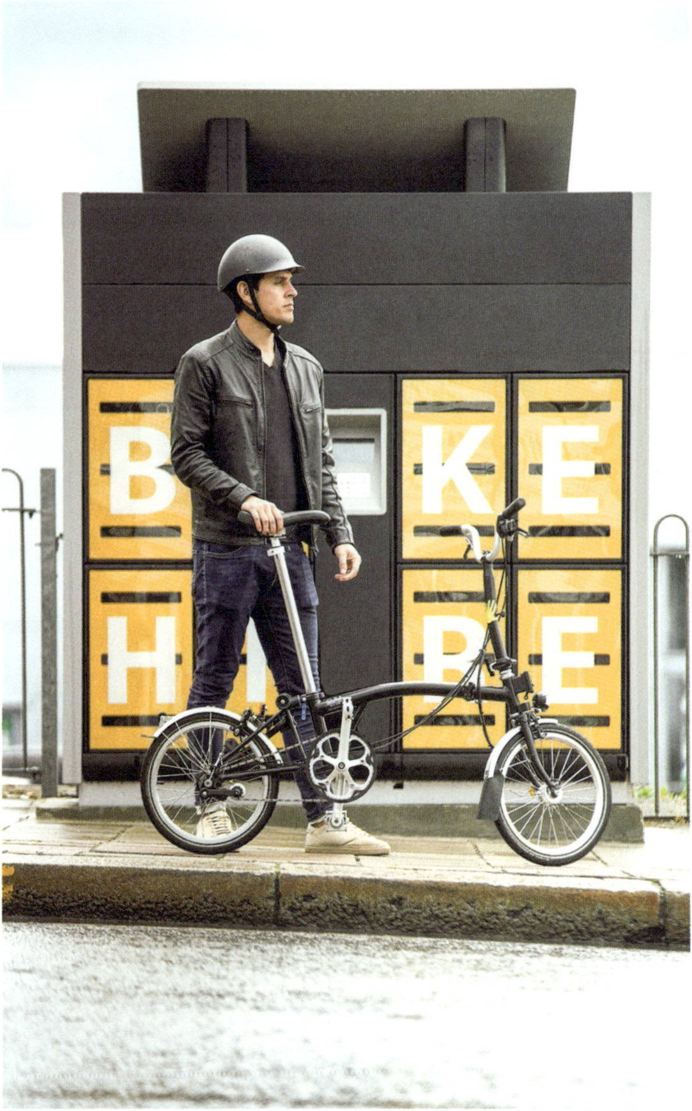

7
OURBIKE

Community cargo bike share scheme

Bike hire has transformed the way we travel around London. But what happens when you have to take your pet for its flea treatment or collect that vintage Moroccan rug you found for a steal on Gumtree? Enter OurBike, whose rentable Babboe Big-E trikes and Ridgeback MK5s are hosted by local businesses from Finsbury Park to Richmond, who make sure they are road-ready. All you have to do is download the app onto your phone, book it, check it and you're off. All for just £3 an hour. Take that, Uber.

Locations across London
ourbike.co.uk

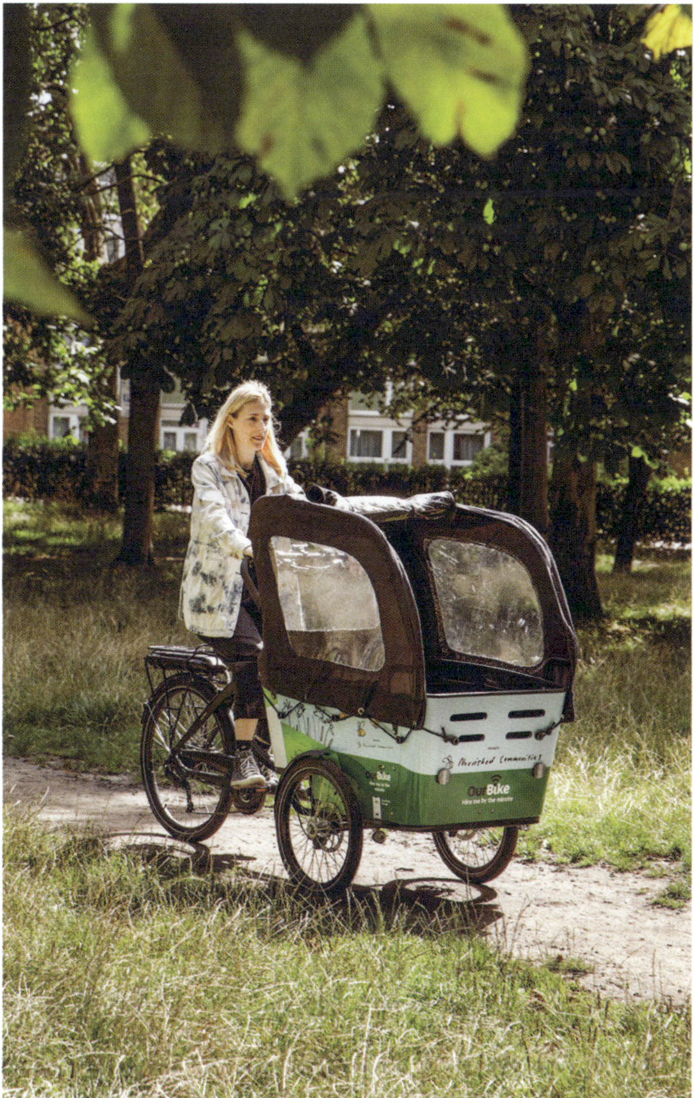
OurBike
Hire me by the minute

8
HUB VÉLO

Small shop winning local hearts

Hub Vélo is more than a shop, it's a community. This Clapton favourite, run by two seriously dedicated cyclists, is the starting point for the Hub Vélo Cycling Club's weekly rides, which anyone can join by signing up to the club. One of the few bike cafes left, serving superior coffee and some seriously moreish cakes, it's also a great shop where you can pick up a brilliant bike or book a service. The pink jersey hanging up is the same one British cyclist Tao Geoghegan Hart was wearing when he won the Giro d'Italia in 2020. A gift from the local hero and one-time regular, it features his signature, with a playful request to switch the cycling club's colours to pink and a heartfelt thank you 'for all your support over the years'.

217 Lower Clapton Road, E5 8EG
Nearest station: Clapton
hub-velo.co.uk

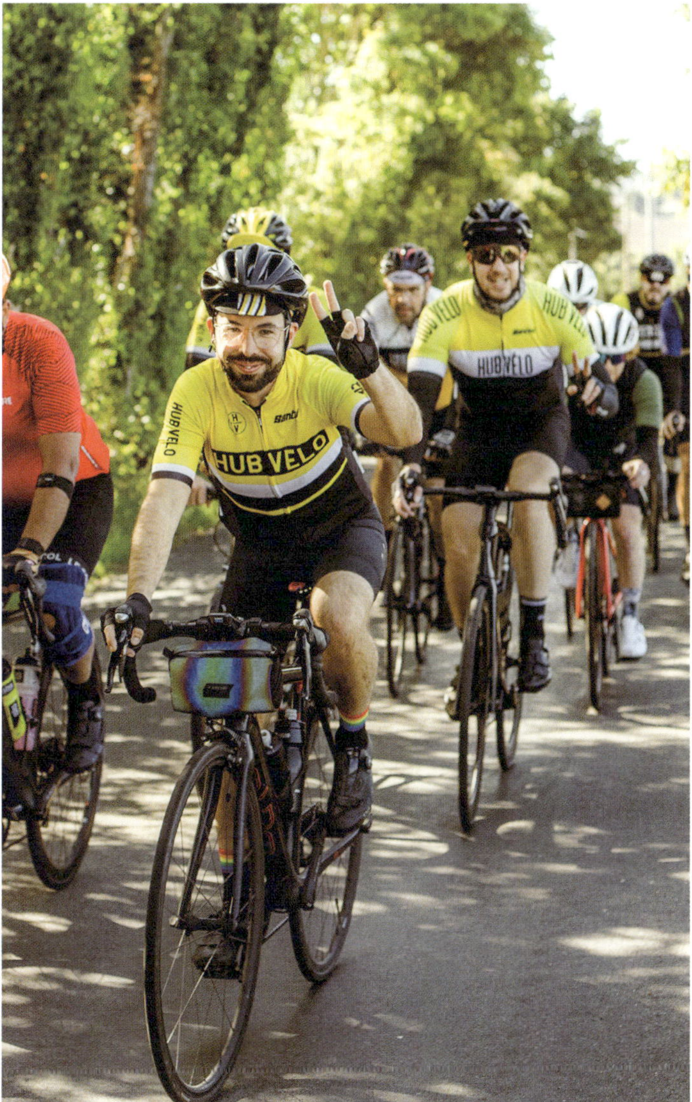
HUB VELO
HUB VELO
HUBVELO

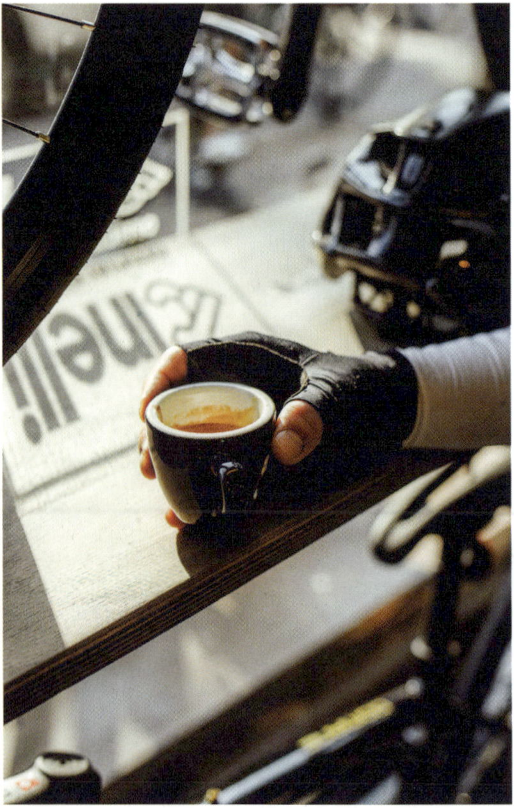

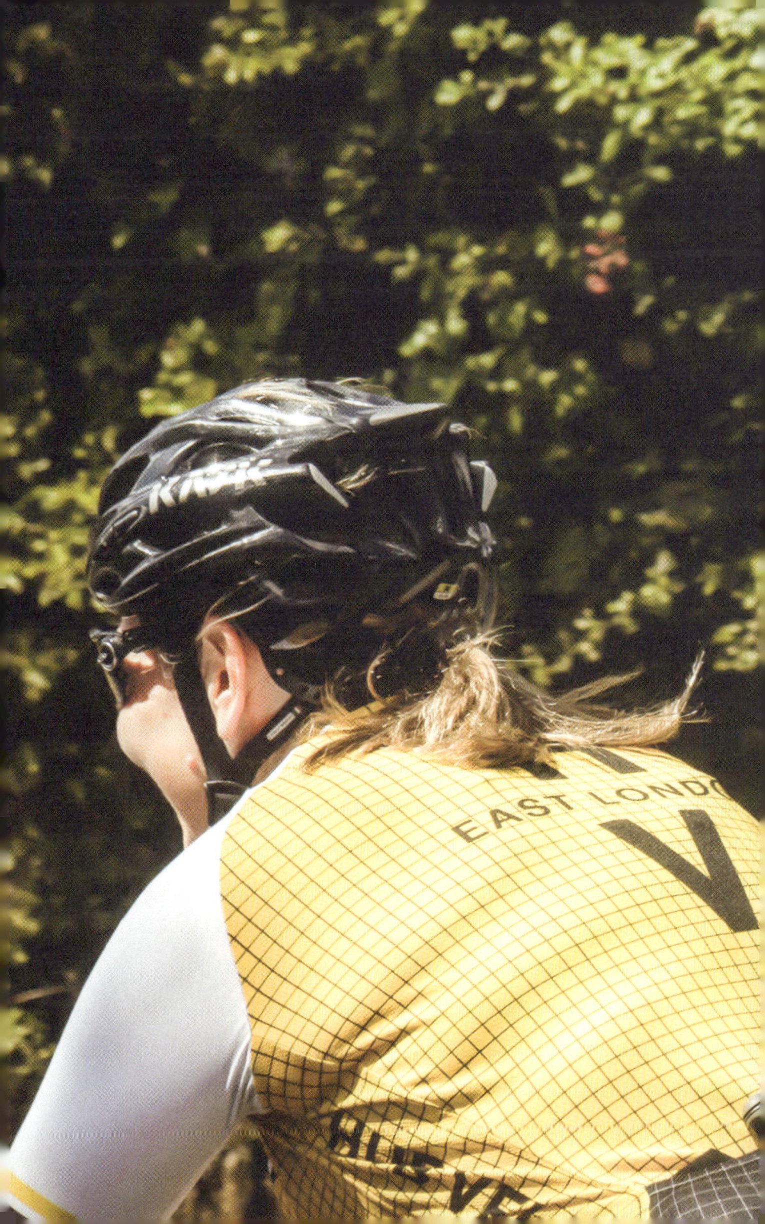
EAST LONDO

9
STAYER

Trailblazing indie brand building forever bikes

East London has a long history of bike-making, but many of the area's old ateliers have been converted to car garages. Today there is a renaissance underway. Judith and Sam, the founders of Stayer, met while studying sculpture at the Slade. Their handsome, stunningly responsive handmade bikes inspire intense devotion among their fan base. Stayer's sought-after frames are expertly welded by Sam (who can trace his family craft back generations), with wheels meticulously constructed by Judith and their small team. A custom or small-batch bike could set you back several grand, but this represents terrific value considering the depth of skill, time and care spent on its creation.

5 Acacia Business Centre, E11 3PJ
Nearest station: Leytonstone High Road
stayercycles.com

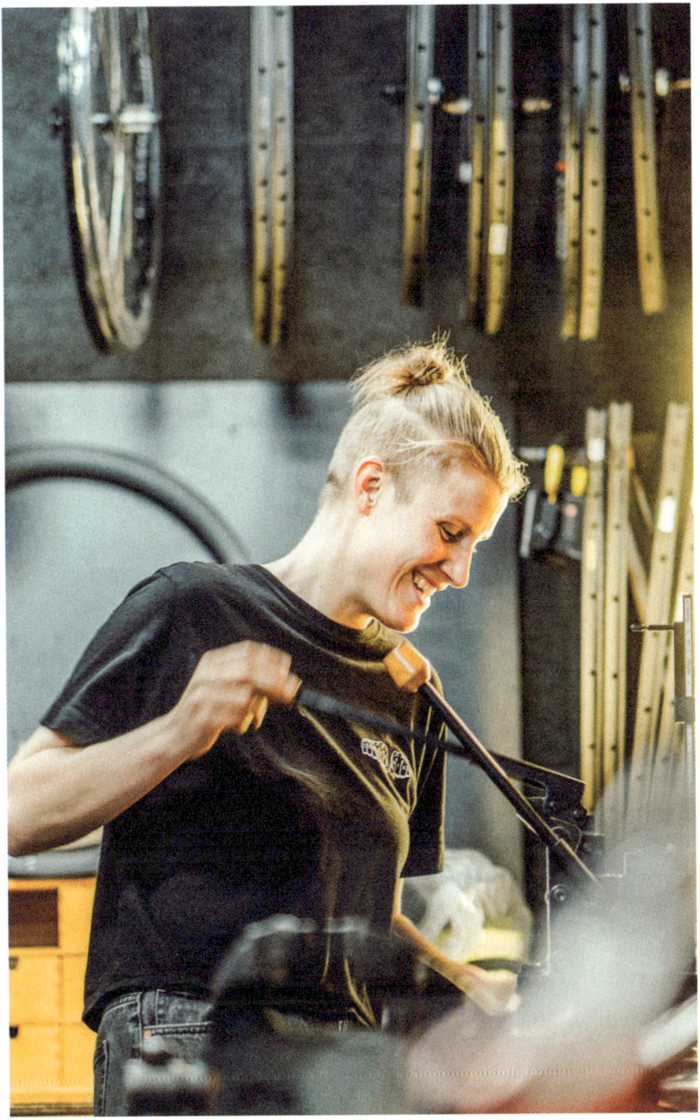

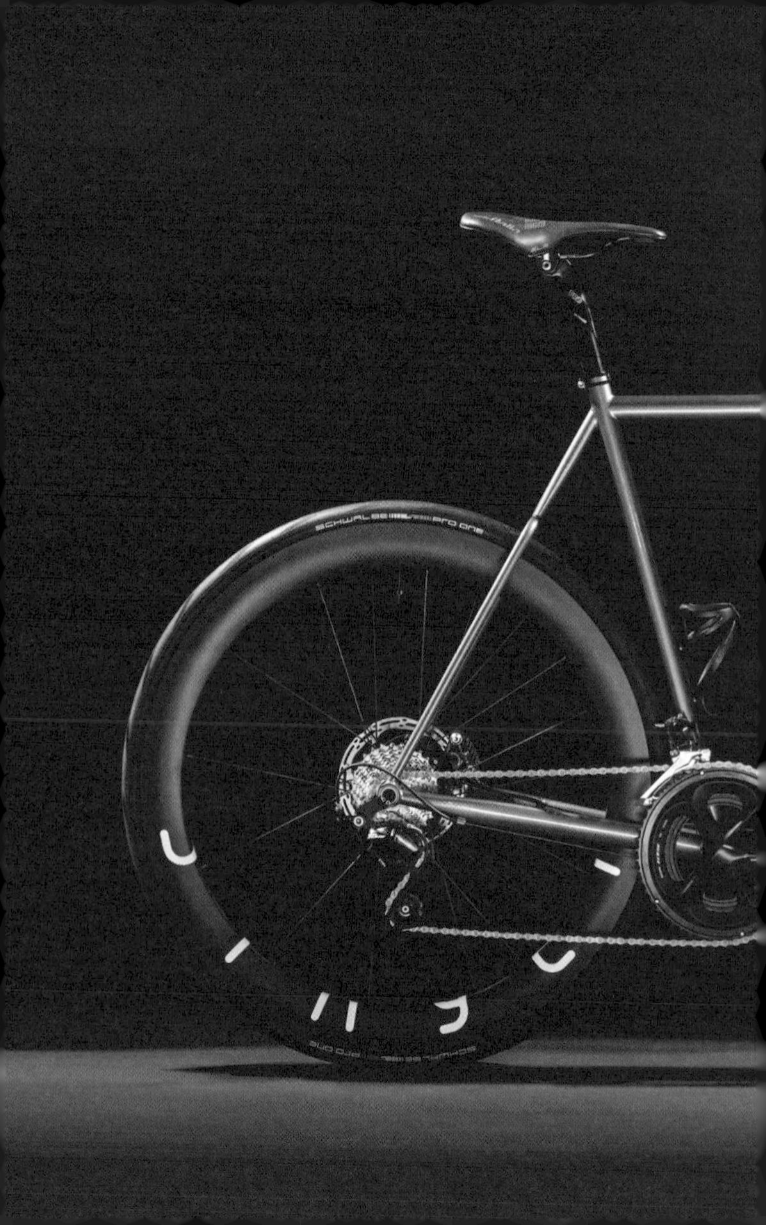
SCHWALBE PRO ONE

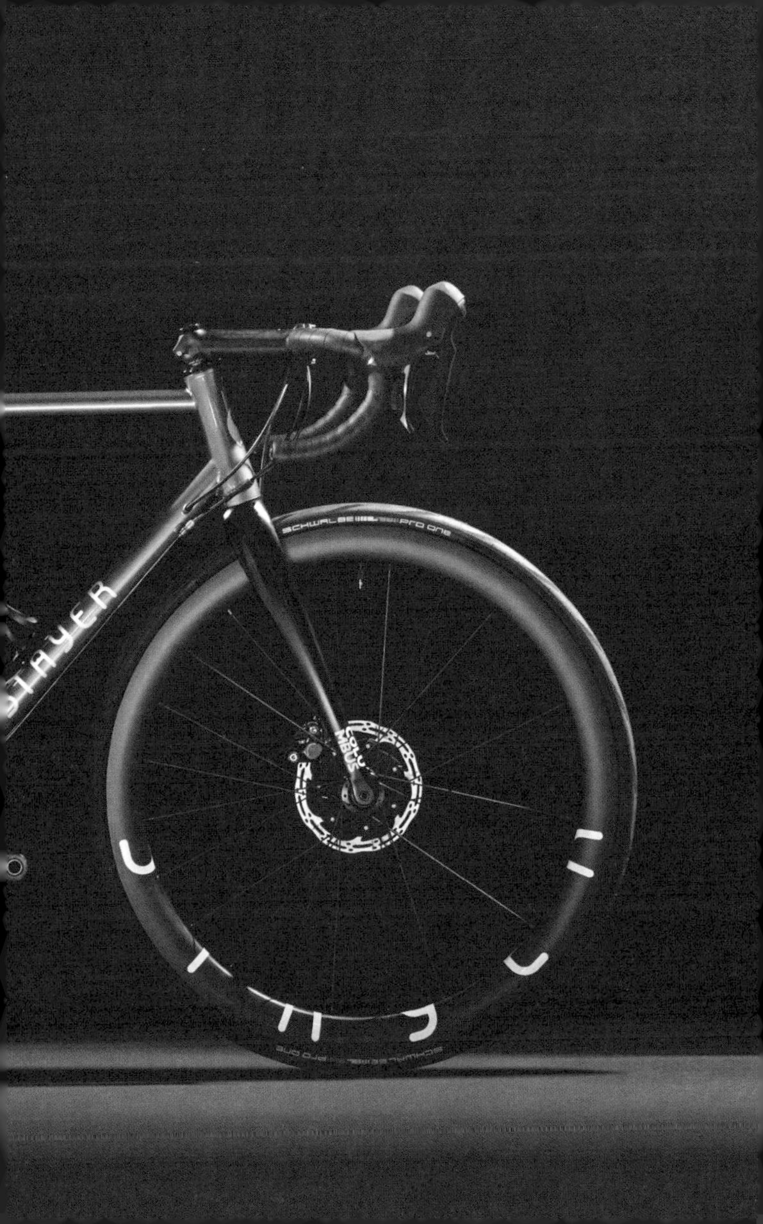
SCHWALBE PRO ONE

10
TEMPLE CYCLES

Going back to the future in style

'Steel is real' is something you hear said more and more often among cyclists. Like vinyl, steel is an old material that's been making a steady come back over the last decade. All bikes were made out of steel until aluminium (which is lighter) and carbon (which is stronger) came to steal steel's throne. But it's the 'realness' of steel that is bringing it back: its longevity and its comfortable ride which, dare we say it, feels more analogue than the precision of carbon. It's also more affordable and, crucially, more repairable. Temple is one of the new steel specialists. Its pared-back design, with retro flourishes, sustainable ethos and gorgeously muted palette, makes it the brand of choice for east London's tastemakers.

240 Brick Lane, E2 7EB
Nearest station: Shoreditch High Street
templecycles.co.uk

240 BRICK LANE
TEMPLE CYCLES
WWW.TEMPLECYCLES.CO.UK
TEMPLE
CYCLES

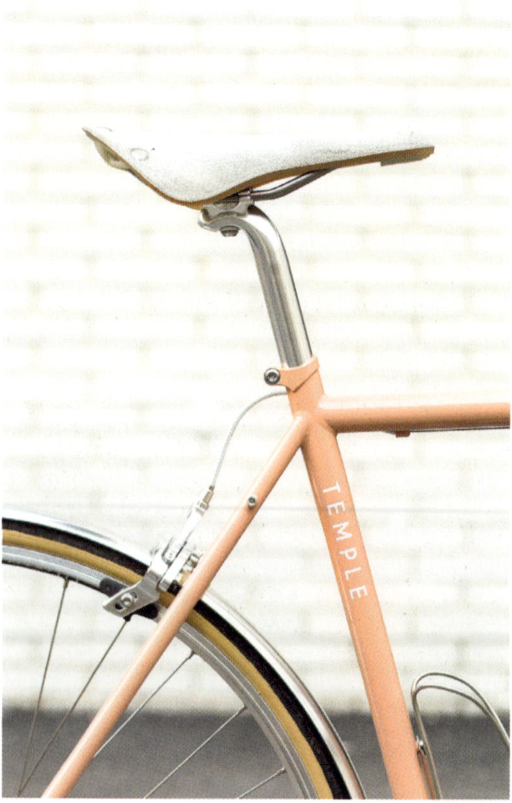
TEMPLE

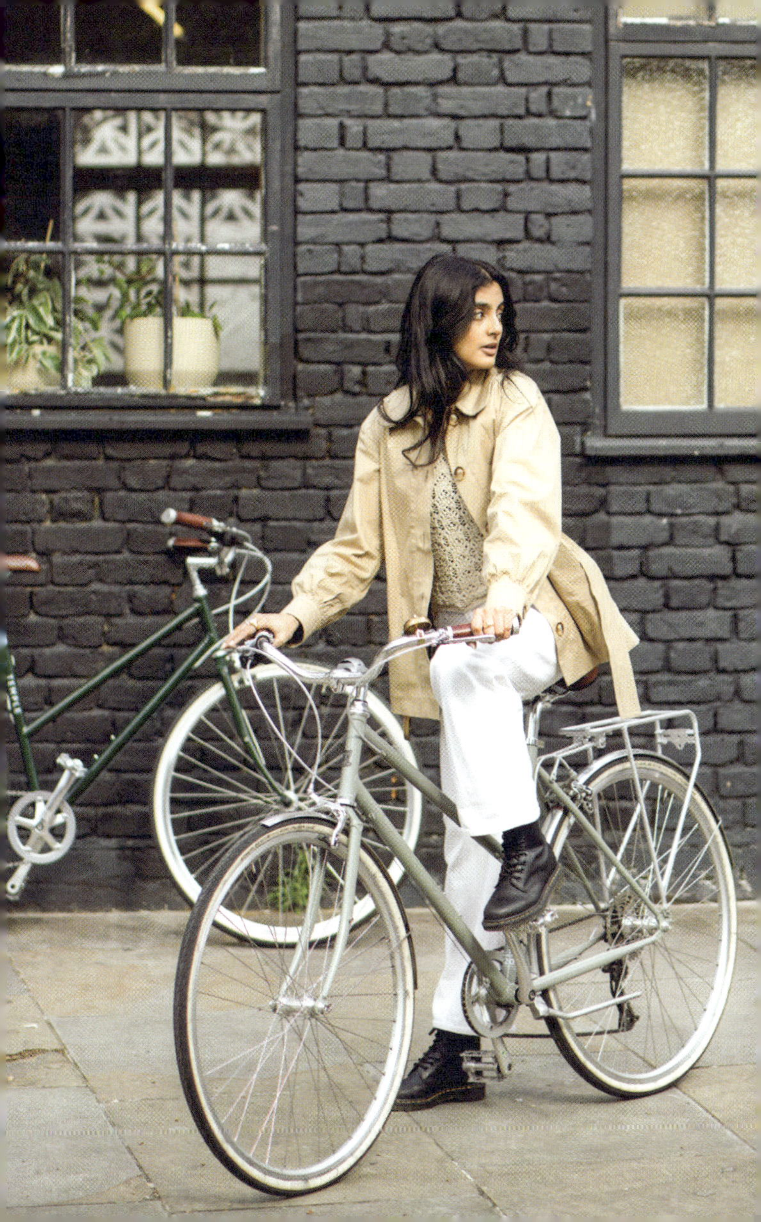

EAST

11
DUNWICH DYNAMO

An unforgettable nocturnal ride

It begins as darkness falls in a pub in London Fields and ends 112 miles later with the sun rising over the Suffolk coast. The Dunwich Dynamo is a magical journey through the night, taking you along winding country lanes, through lush forests and finally to the sea. Starting out in 1992 as a ride organised by the London School of Cycling, it's still only semi-official and that's its charm. You'll find riders of all kinds and abilities. Some play music from speakers, others festoon their bikes with fairy lights. Speed is not the point. Along the route, pop-up pit stops offer delicious snacks to keep energy and spirits up. DD, as it's affectionately known, is a ride like no other.

From Pub on the Park, Martello Street,
E8 3PE to Dunwich Beach
Nearest station: London Fields
dunwichdynamo.co.uk

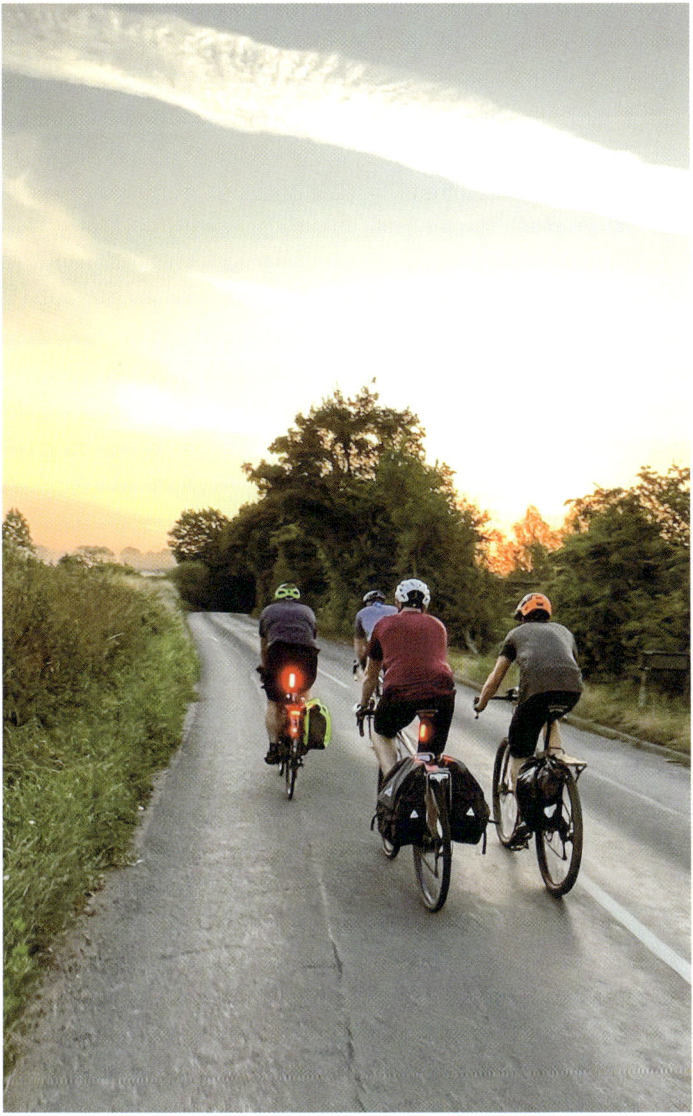

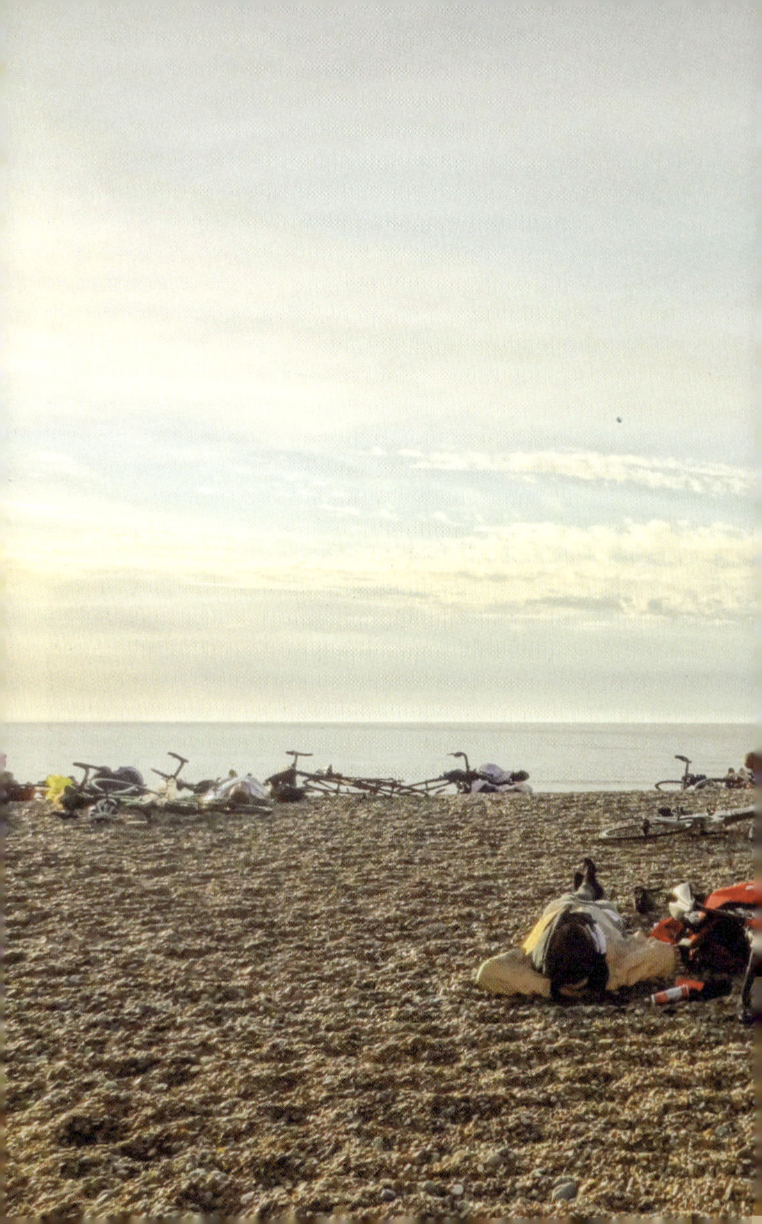

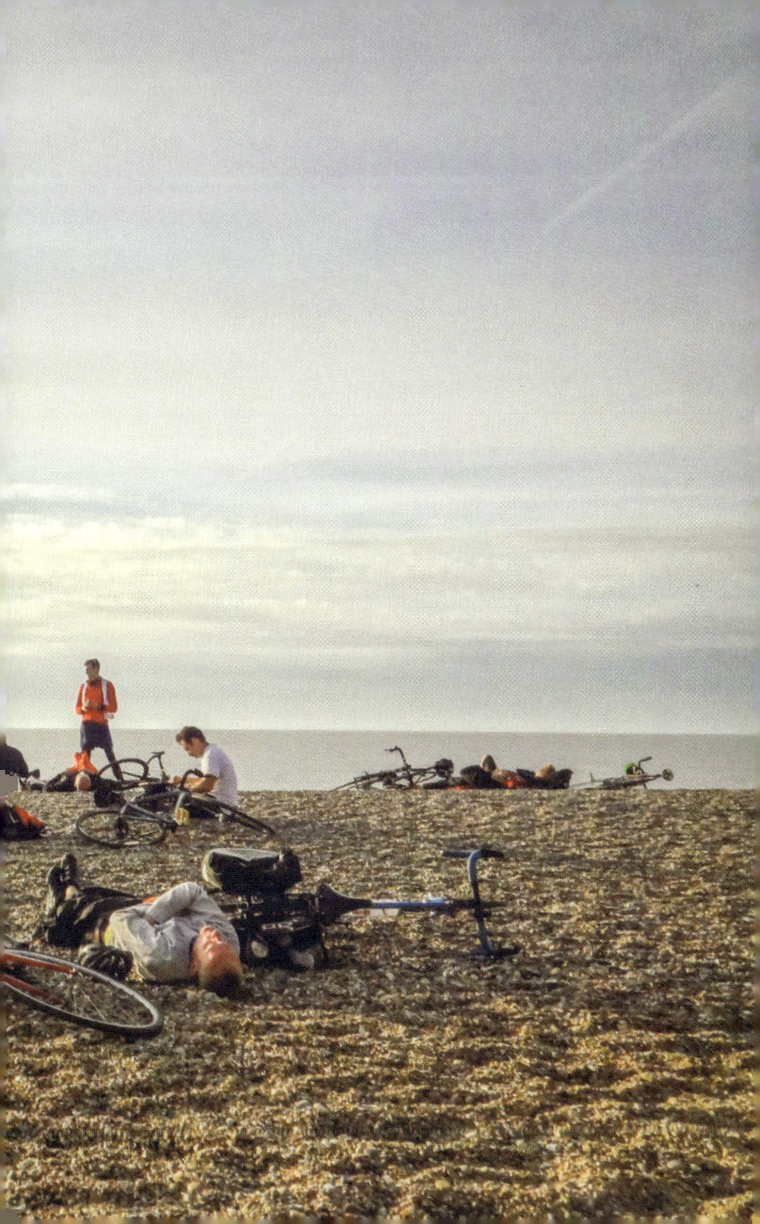

12
LEE VALLEY VELOPARK

Follow in the tracks of Olympians

What a summer it was. Who can forget those eight glorious gold medals that sent GB cyclists to the top of the table in the 2012 Summer Olympics? It was on this very spot that the track and BMX races took place, in an award-winning, elegant, curved building designed by Ron Webb. Today, cyclists of all types flock to the VeloPark to use the BMX track, one-mile road course, eight-mile mountain bike trail and velodrome. For around £50, anyone over 12 can book a taster session to sample the thrill of a flying lap. But you'd better keep up the pace if you don't want to find yourself sliding down the steep, slippery sides of the track!

Abercrombie Road,
Queen Elizabeth Olympic Park, E20 3AB
Nearest station: Stratford
better.org.uk/leisure-centre/lee-valley/velopark

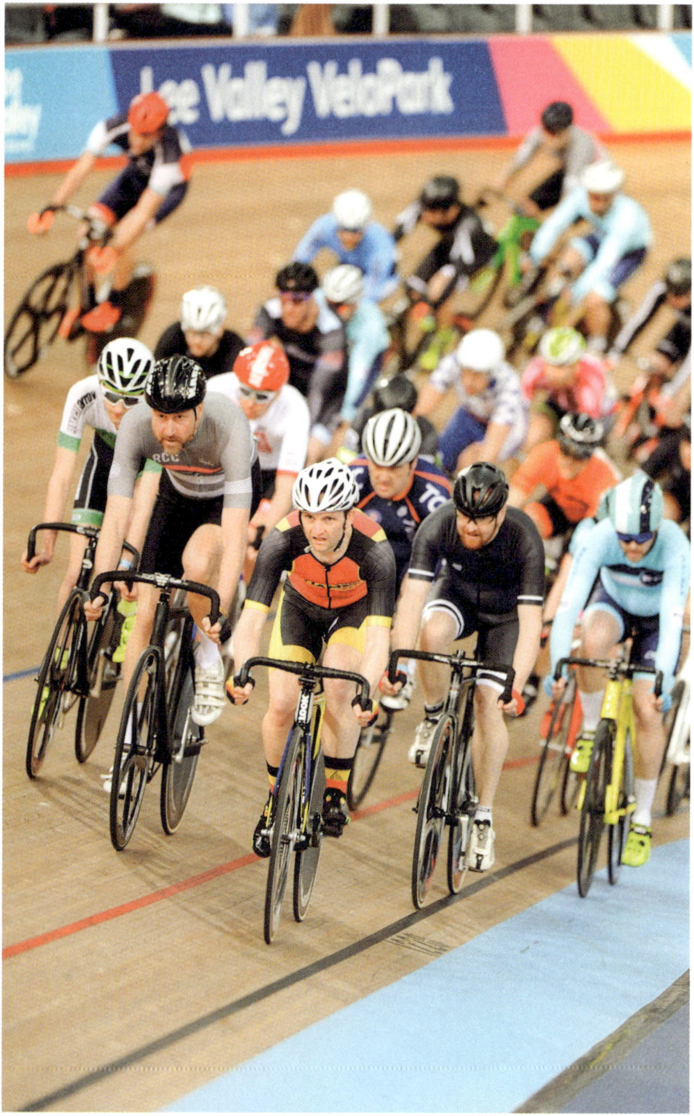
ee Valley VeloPark

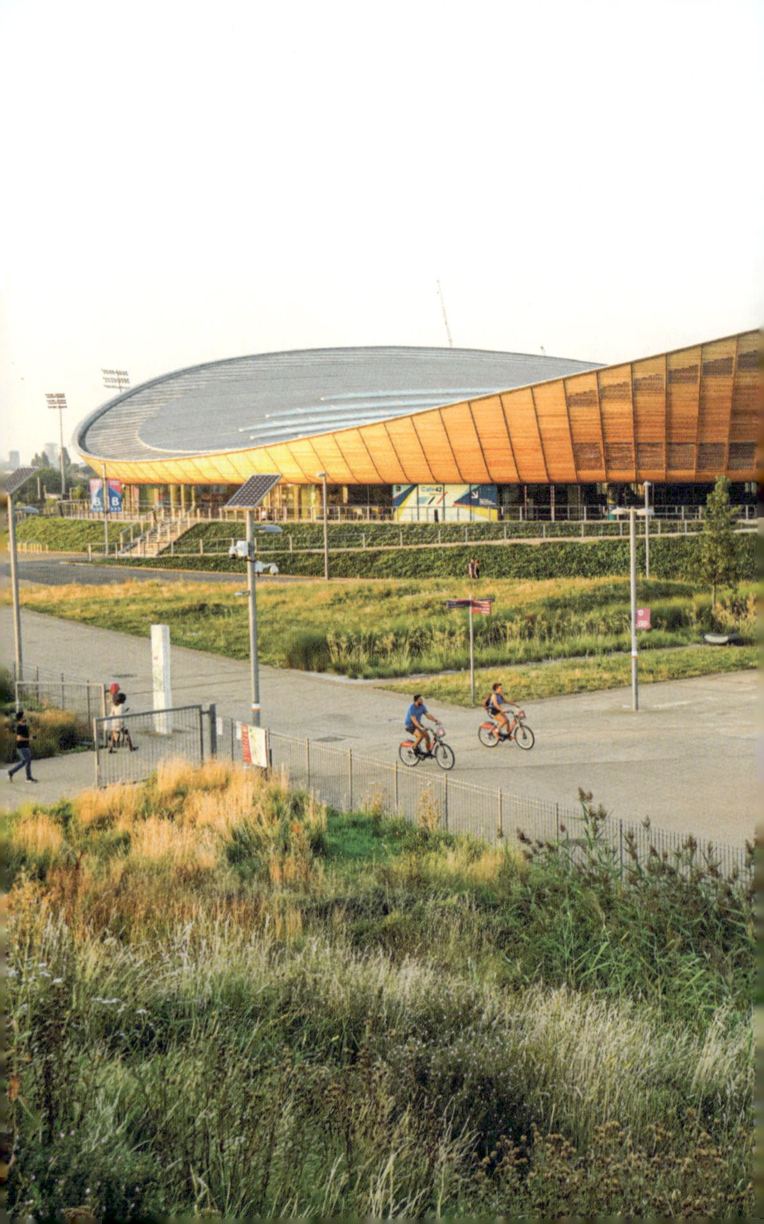

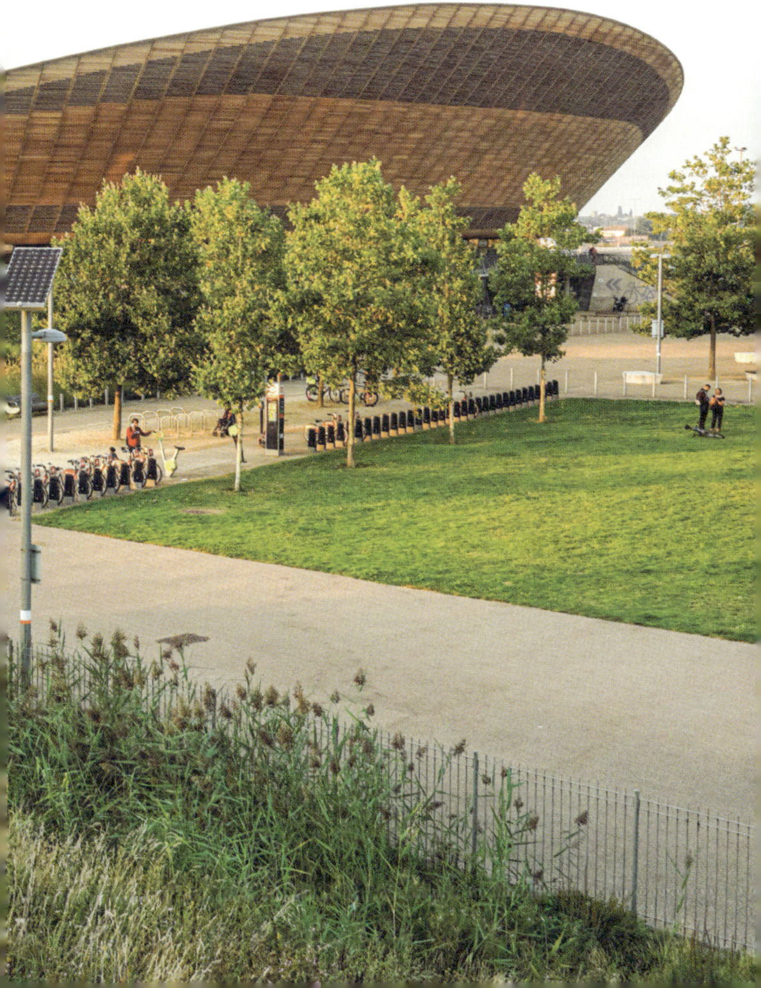

13

BLACK UNITY BIKE RIDE

Celebrating London's Black cycling communities

Dubbed 'Carnival on bikes', Black Unity Bike Ride is an annual 14-mile cycle across London, bringing together more than 20 grassroots collectives from across the city. In between are monthly Come Ride With Us-led indoor rides at the Lee Valley VeloPark (no.12). Partnered with Rapha (no.27), Sport England and others, they've been on a mission since 2020 to showcase the diversity of the city's cycling scene and to inspire more Black cyclists, currently under-represented in the sport. Some 2,000 riders showed up for the 2022 sportive – a joyful day promoting love, community, wellness and a narrative shift about what it means to be a London cyclist.

blackunitybikeride.com

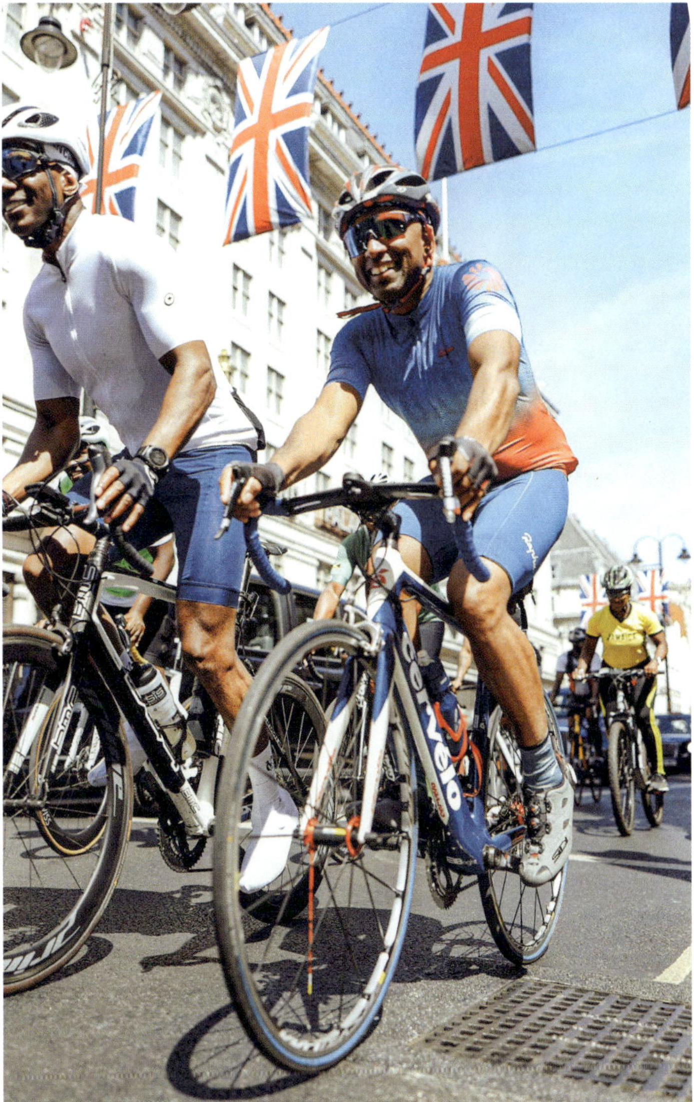

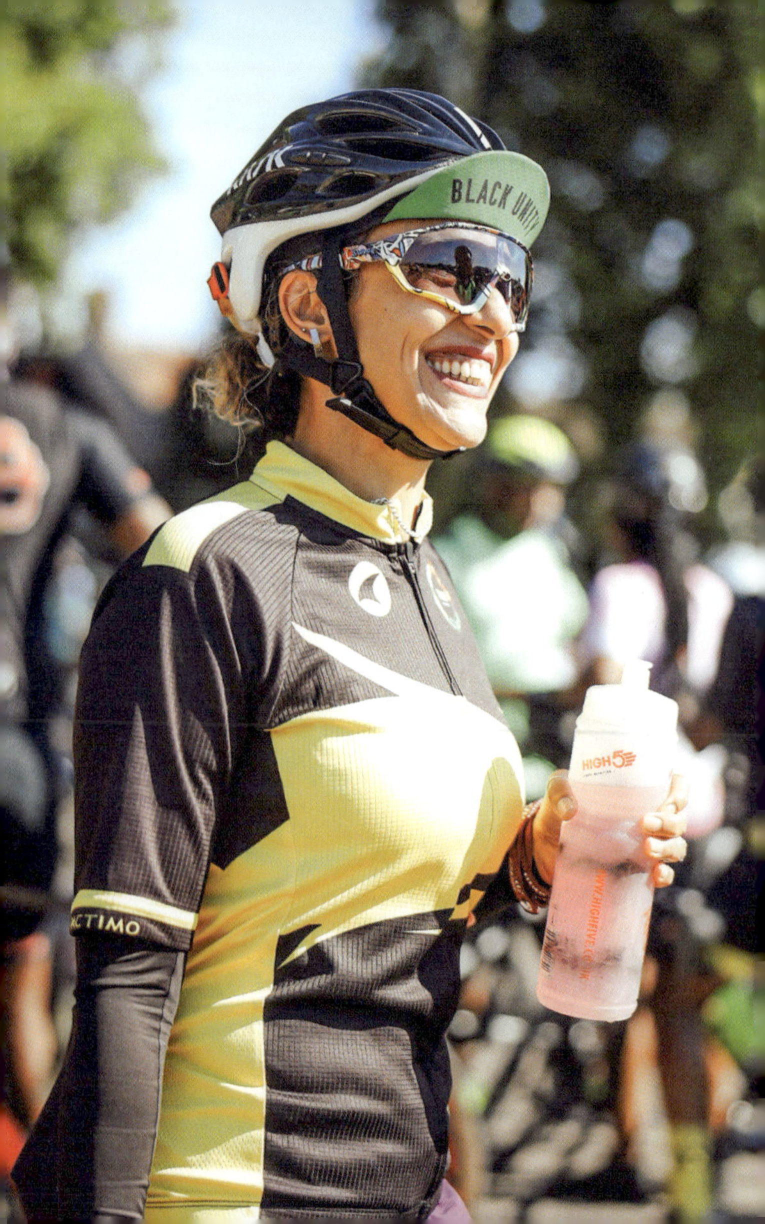

BLACK UNITY
HIGH5
CTIMO

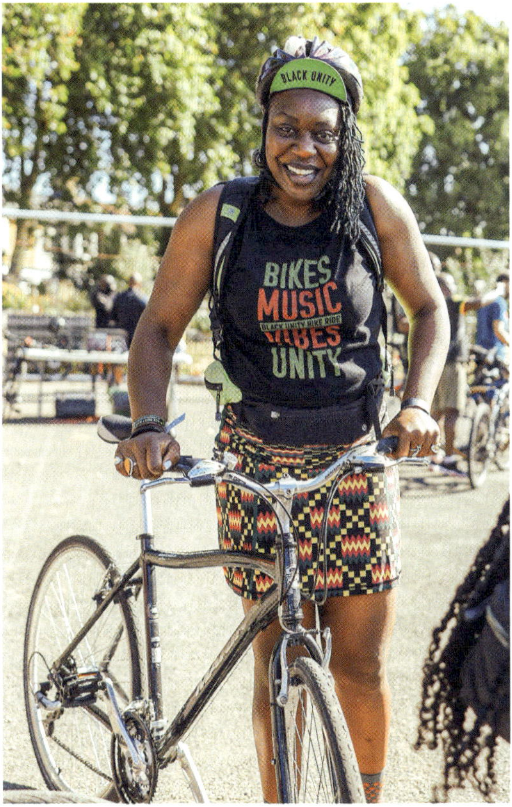
BLACK UNITY
BIKES
MUSIC
BLACK UNITY BIKE RIDE
UNITY

14
FREDDIE GRUBB

Sophisticated retro-style bikes

Before setting up Freddie Grubb in 2015, Malcolm Harding had built up several decades of experience in furniture design. Add to this an appreciation for the panache and exceptional build quality of vintage bikes – he's a proud collector of antique bicycles, including a tandem from 1934 – and you have the secret to Freddie Grubb's success. These charming London-made city bicycles are all about the flourishes. The traditional leather saddle. The oh-so-subtle branding. The sleek frames, offering the clean look normally reserved for single speed bikes but actually with up to eight gears. These are Instagram-worthy future heirlooms your grandchildren will cherish in years to come.

27 Gossamer Gardens, E2 9FN
Nearest station: Cambridge Heath
freddiegrubb.com

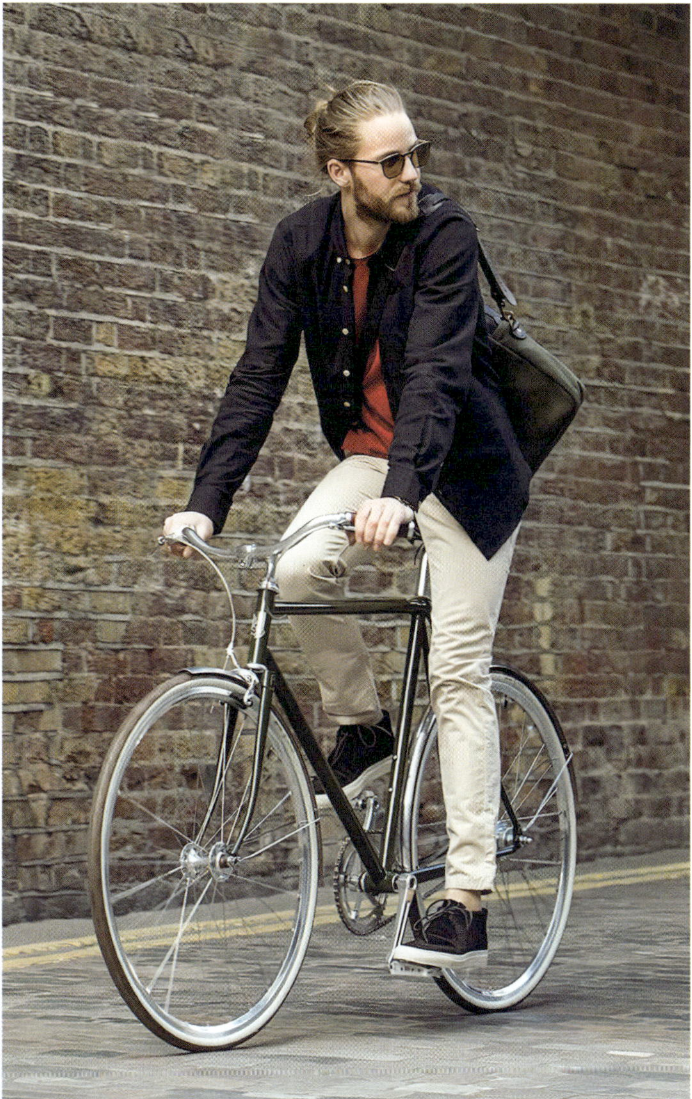

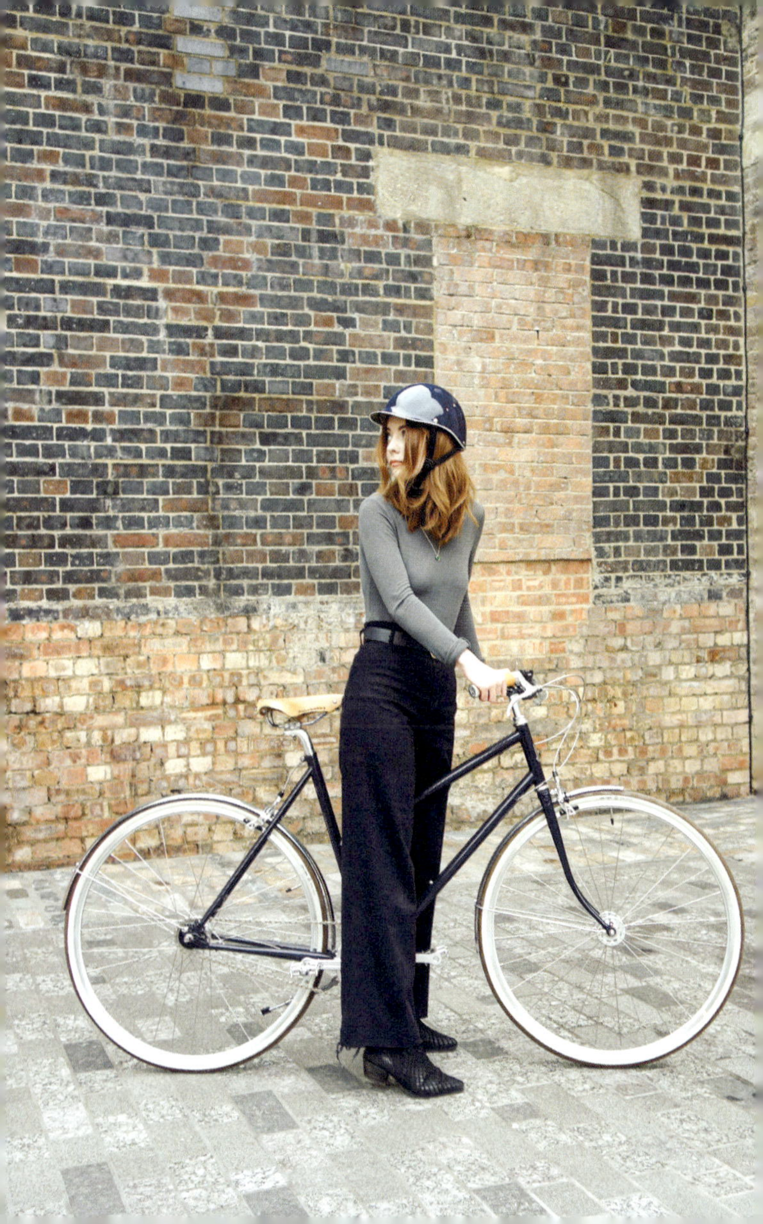

FREDDIE GRUBB

15
QUIRK CYCLES
Ultra desirable custom-made steel bikes

To Rob Quirk, frame building is alchemy – a metallurgical process combining base metals to conjure something extraordinary. Rob's background is in ultra-distance racing (anything longer than 100 miles) – a big draw for many customers – and in the past he would design a bike with a specific race in mind. This was at a time when mainstream brands were marketing bikes with Olympians' names, even though that didn't reflect the reality for most riders. The original gravel bikes, now such a popular kind of cycling, were pioneered by bespoke makers like Quirk, proving the best bikes and ideas come from small independents. A bespoke Quirk bicycle is also an object of immense beauty, with marbled finishes that will occupy your daydreams.

86 Wallis Road, E9 5LN
Nearest station: Hackney Wick
quirkcycles.com

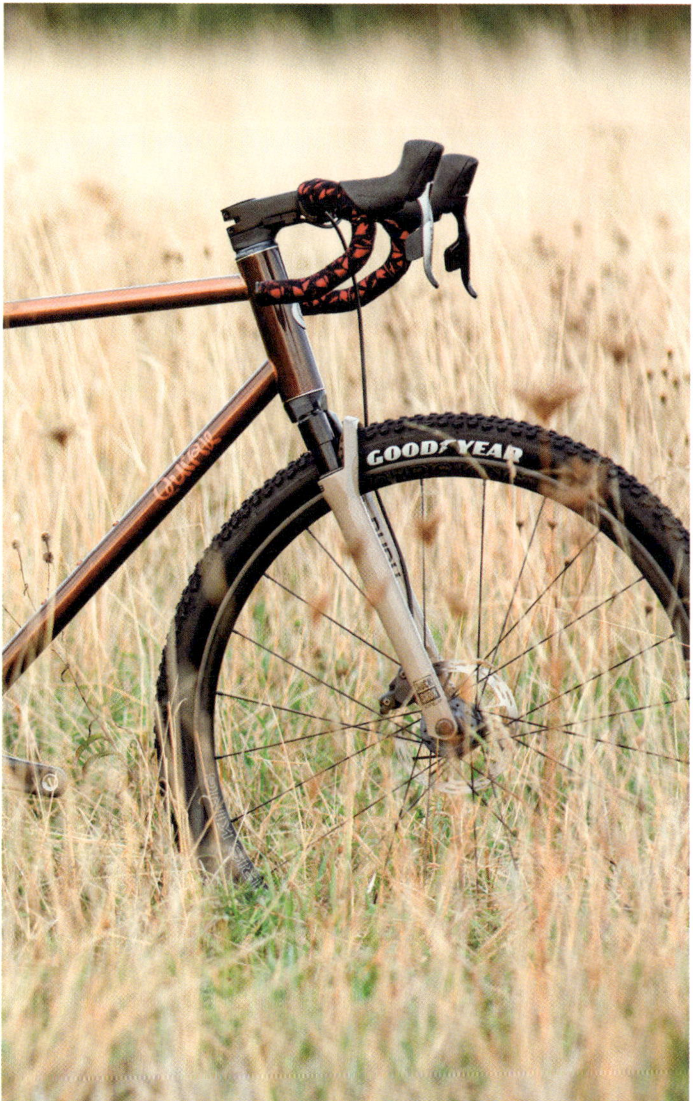
GOODYEAR

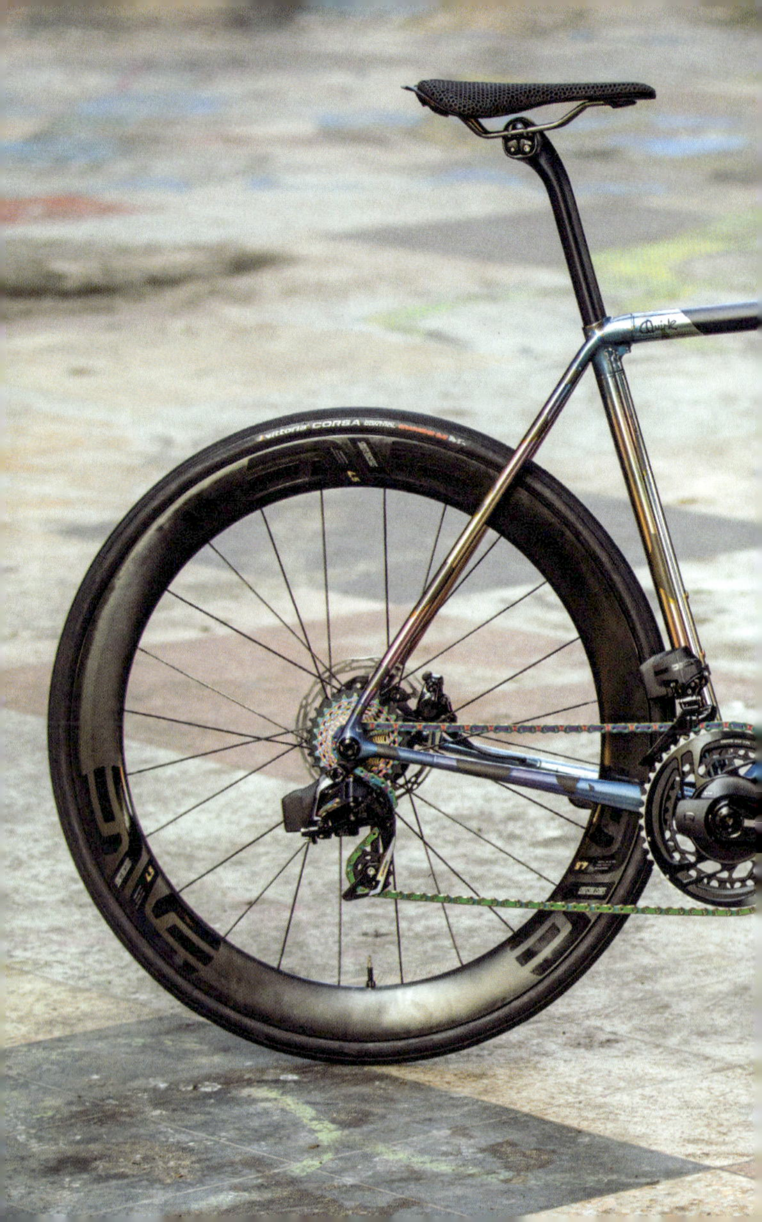
vittoria CORSA CONTROL

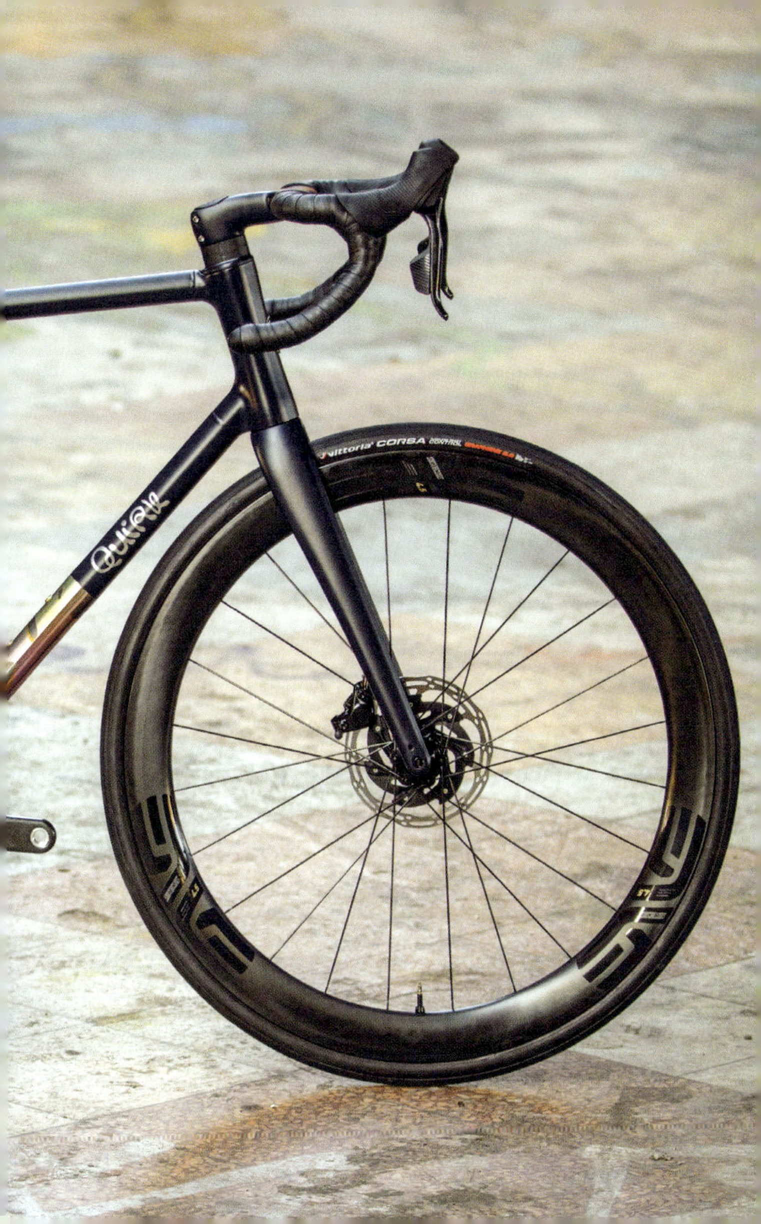
Vittoria CORSA

16

BURGESS PARK BMX TRACK

Ride with Peckham's champion BMXers

BMX was born on the dirt tracks of 1970s California, but today you'll spot BMXers around the world. There's a thriving scene here in London, with BMX tracks in every corner of the capital. This one is home to the Peckham BMX Club, who've notched up a number of British, European and World championship wins, and count Olympic silver medallist Kye Whyte – aka the Prince of Peckham – among their own. You don't have to be a member to sample the gravity-defying thrill of BMXing on these slopes, though. Anyone can join a free 'rock up and ride' session once you've completed an induction.

Burgess Park, Albany Road, SE5 0AH
Nearest stations: Peckham Rye, Elephant & Castle
peckhambmx.co.uk

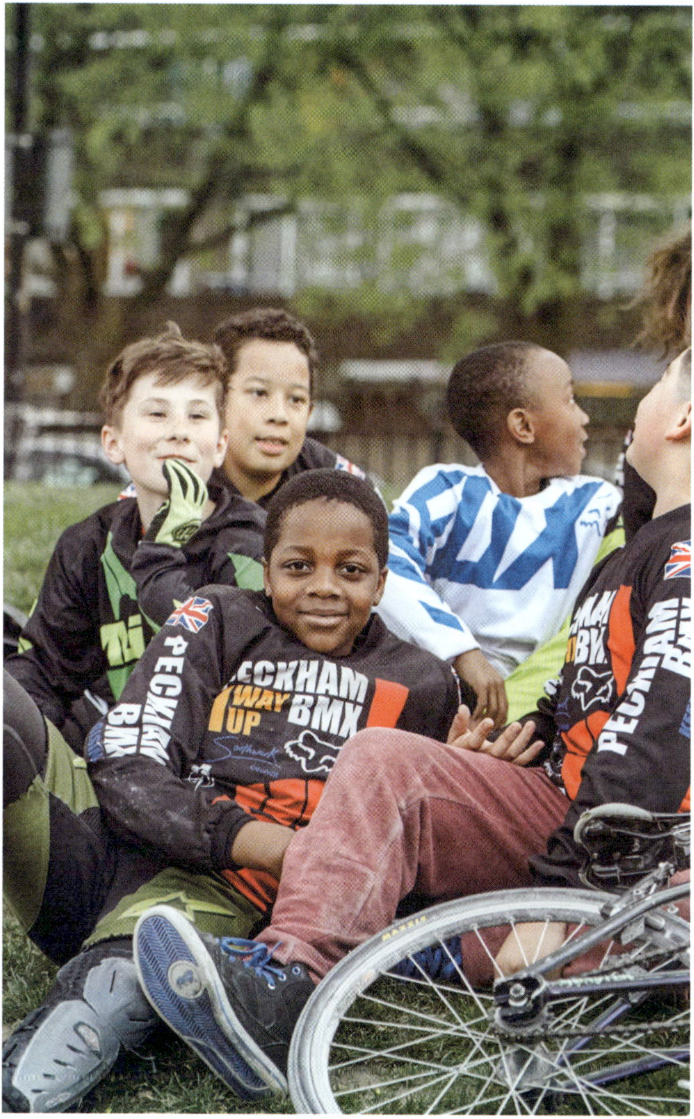
ECKHAM
WAY
UP
BMX
PECKHAM
BMX

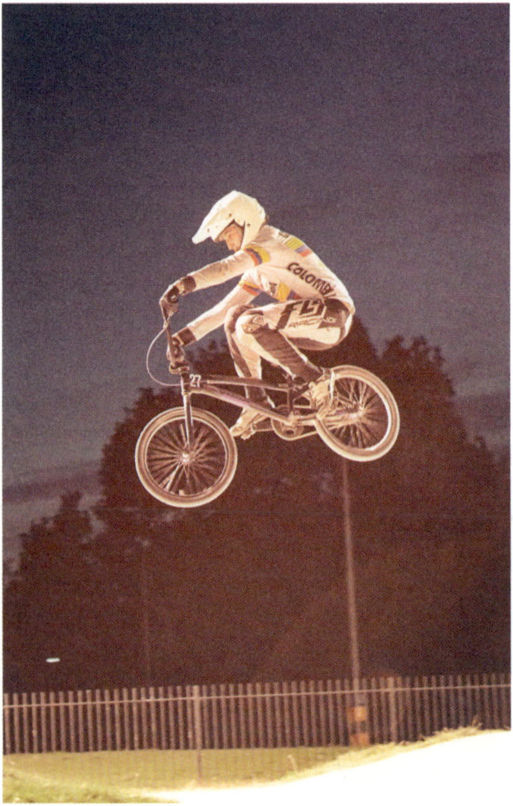

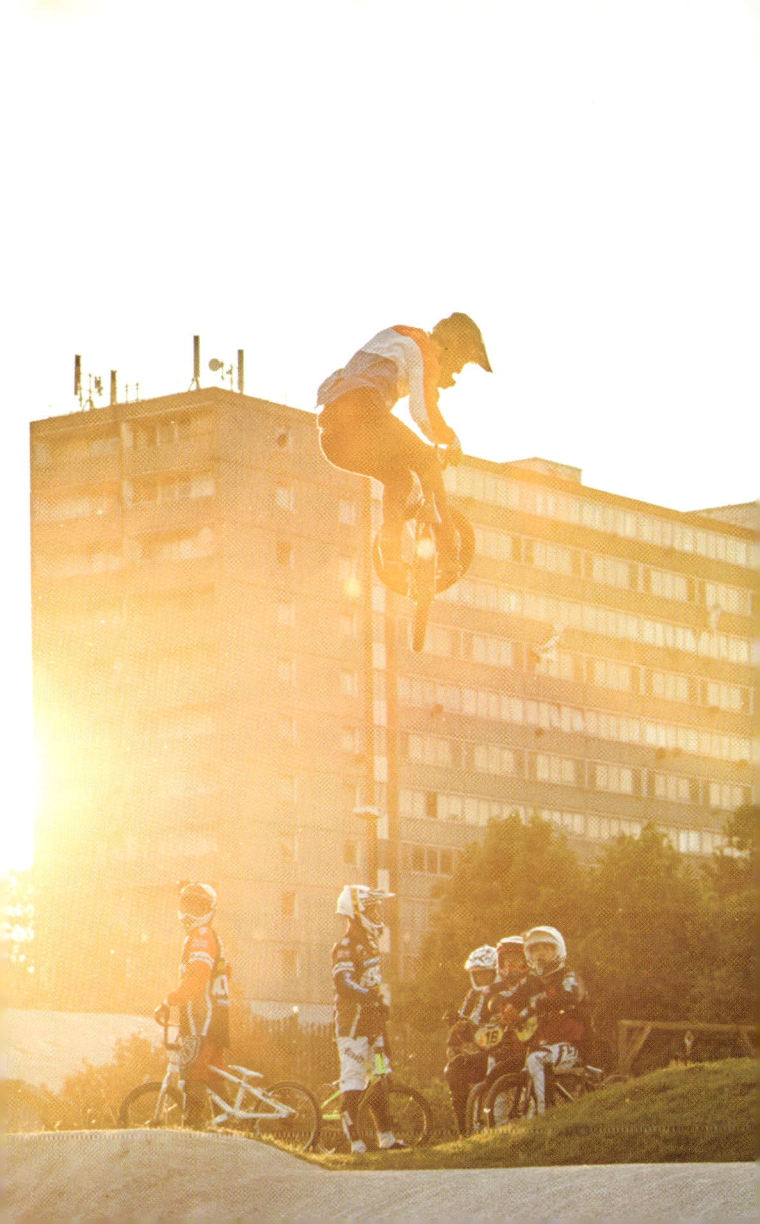

17

THE BIKE PROJECT

Pre-loved bikes that help refugee cyclists

Getting around London is not cheap. A TfL Travelcard can cost £15 a day whereas, once you have your bike, lock and helmet, cycling is free. The Bike Project's mission is to help refugees reap the benefits of cycling by giving them pre-loved bikes fixed up in their Deptford workshop. But they keep some bikes back to sell here and online, to help fund this work. You'll find some incredible bargains – high quality bikes by reputable brands alongside accessories that include brand new jerseys donated by the good people at Rapha and sold for a fraction of the price. Since 2013, the charity has donated more than 11,000 refurbished bikes, each one bringing its new owner the freedom of cycling.

170-172 Camberwell Road, SE5 0EE
Nearest station: Denmark Hill
thebikeproject.co.uk

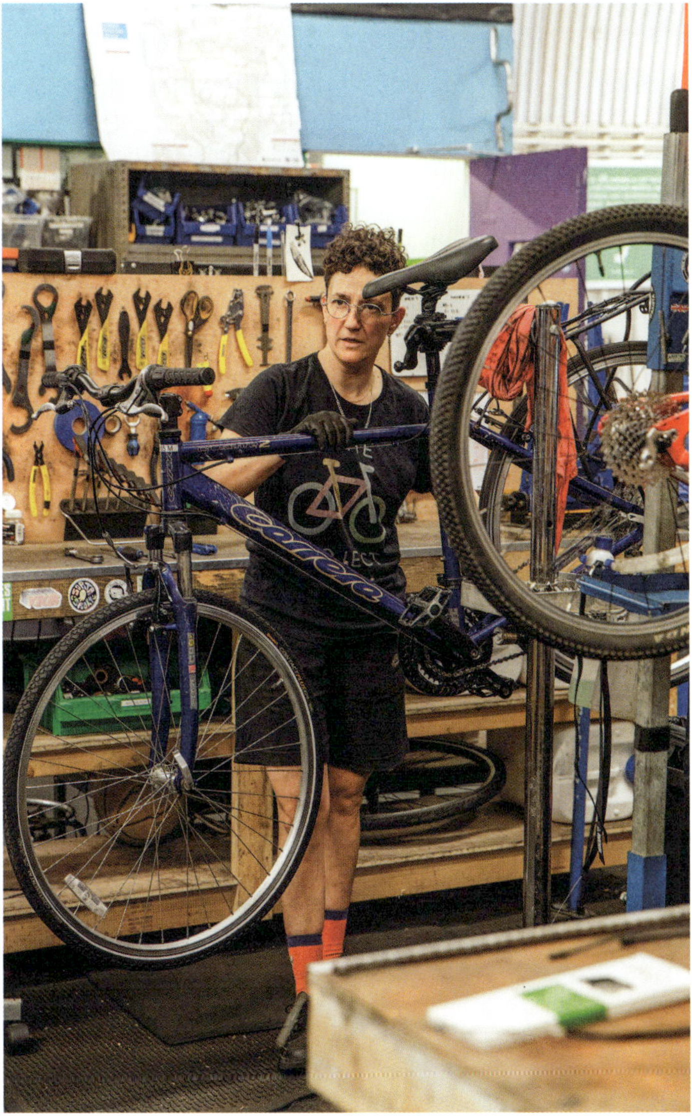
Carrera

18
NIPNIP

Mobile mechanics on two wheels

We've all been there. Almost at work after pedalling through the London traffic when the bike decides it's not playing. Instead of dragging it to the closest bike shop, which may not be particularly close, you can now summon NipNip's emergency bike repair service. They'll rock up, trailer in tow, and fix it. Alternatively, they can take it to one of their three London workshops, where a mechanic will revive it. A few companies are doing something similar, but NipNip is the best. Because their mechanics are highly skilled and properly passionate, they will take really good care of your bike. You can opt for a same-day service, and they'll even lend you a free courtesy bike while you wait.

nipnip.co.uk
172 Great Suffolk Street, SE1 1PE

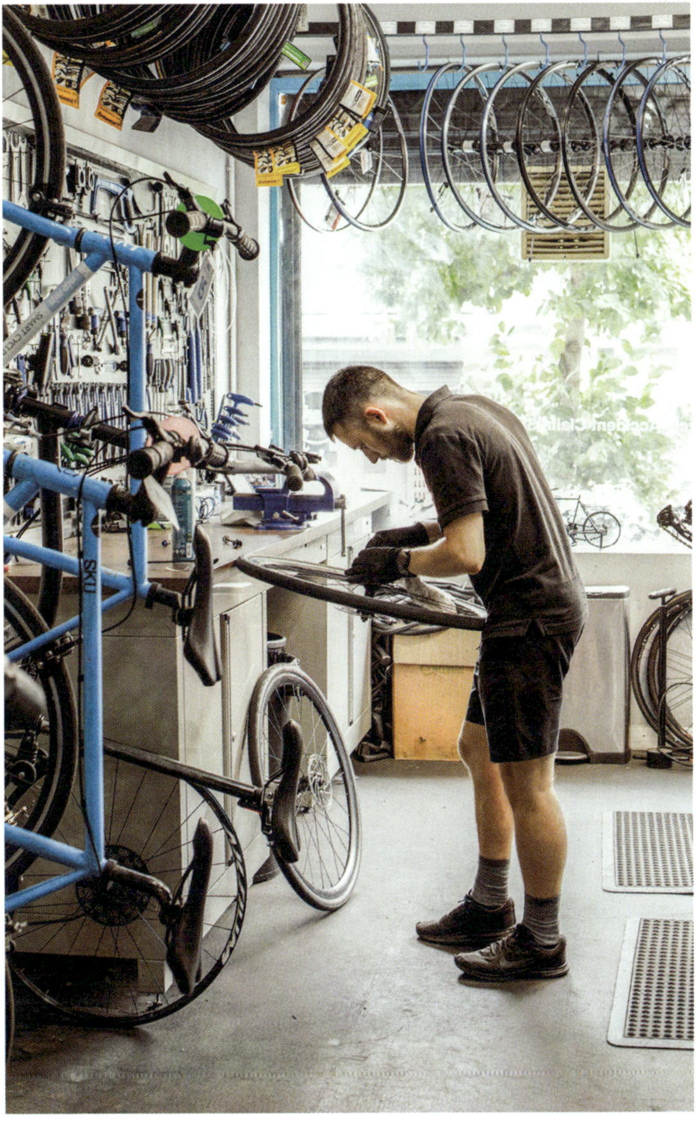
SKU

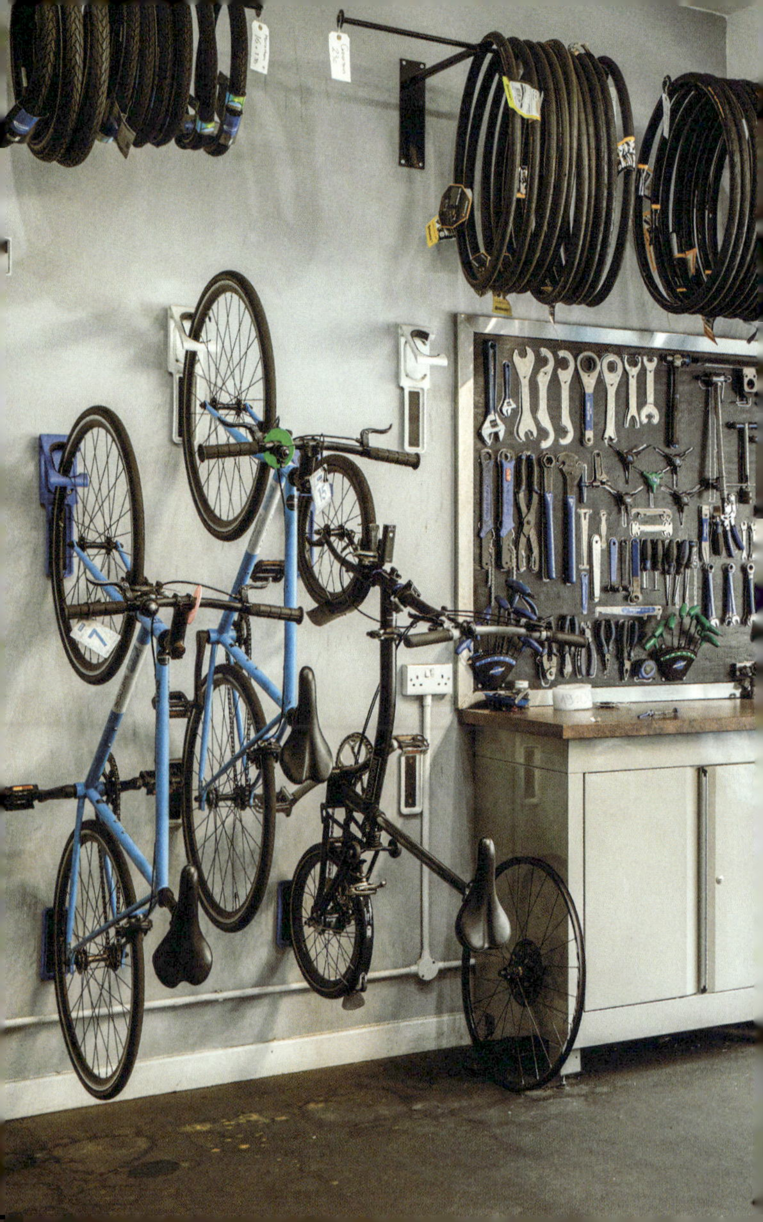

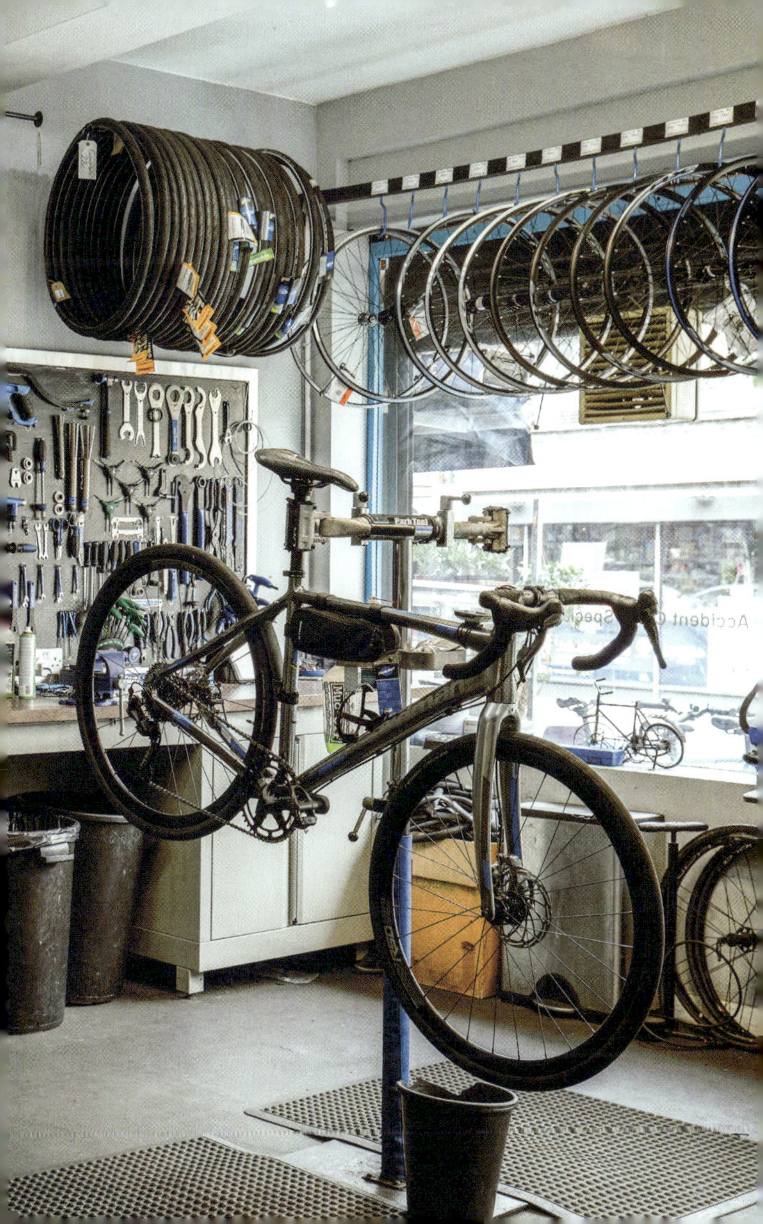
ParkTool

19

THE DYNAMO

Bikes, brunch and pizza

The upcycled signage fashioned from old bikes tells you that you'll be among friends here. This hangout – popular with south London cycle clubs, including Clapham Cycling and London Dynamo – serves artisanal coffee from Caravan Coffee Roasters, fancy fry-ups, pizzas and more, as well as hosting indoor cycling evenings and screening races. Grab a table in the industrial-feel interior space or kick back on the outdoor terrace if the weather is amenable. No need to worry whether your wheels are safe while you indulge, as there's secure indoor bike parking on-site. This is a choice spot to meet after a ride in Richmond Park or for a leisurely beer with bike pals.

200–204 Putney Bridge Road, SW15 2NA
Nearest station: Putney Bridge
the-dynamo.co.uk

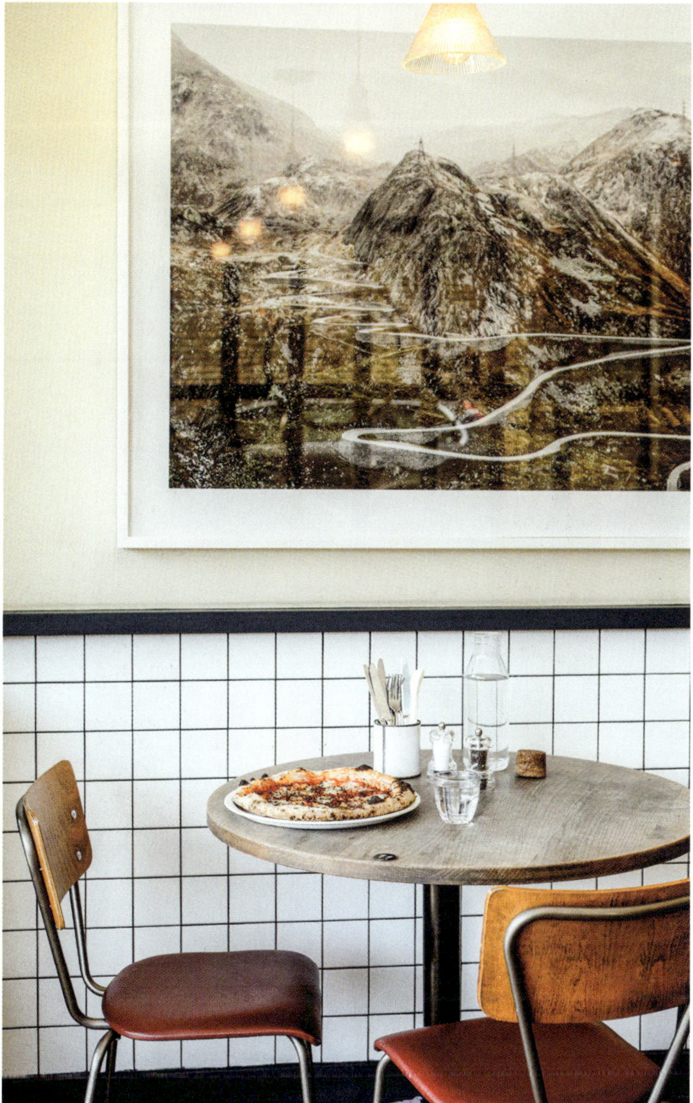

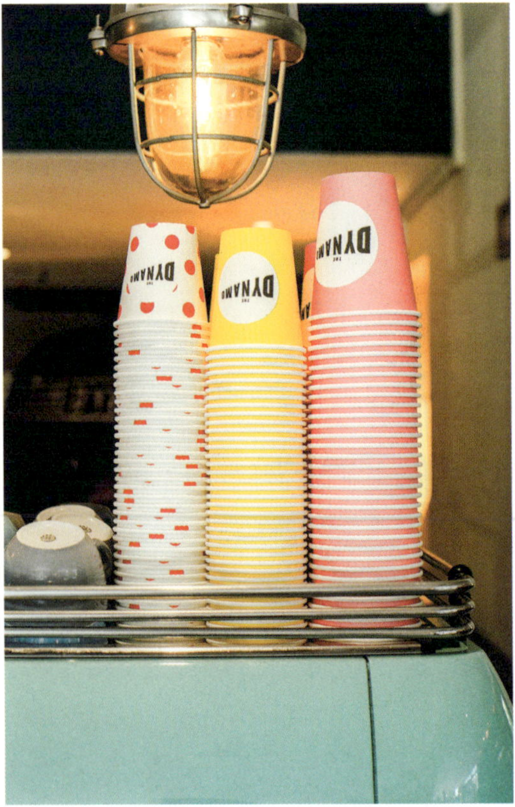
DYNAMO
DYNAMO
DYNAMO

THE DYNAMO

COFFEE • BREAKFASTS & BRUNCHES

SOUTH

20

HERNE HILL VELODROME

A powerhouse of grassroots cycling

Where to even begin? It's hard to do justice to Herne Hill Velodrome, the epicentre of community cycling south of the river. Literally any initiative you could name is happening here, including instruction for two-year-olds to adults, leagues for every type of racer (including the UK's biggest women's league) and accessible cycling for people with disabilities run by Wheels for Wellbeing. Open since 1891, this is a site steeped in cycling history, having hosted track cycling events for the 1948 Olympics. Don't miss the annual South London Grand Prix, where you can watch elite riders and rising young stars of the sport from across the country turn into a blur as they shoot around the track.

104 Burbage Road, SE24 9HE
Nearest stations: North Dulwich, Herne Hill
hernehillvelodrome.com

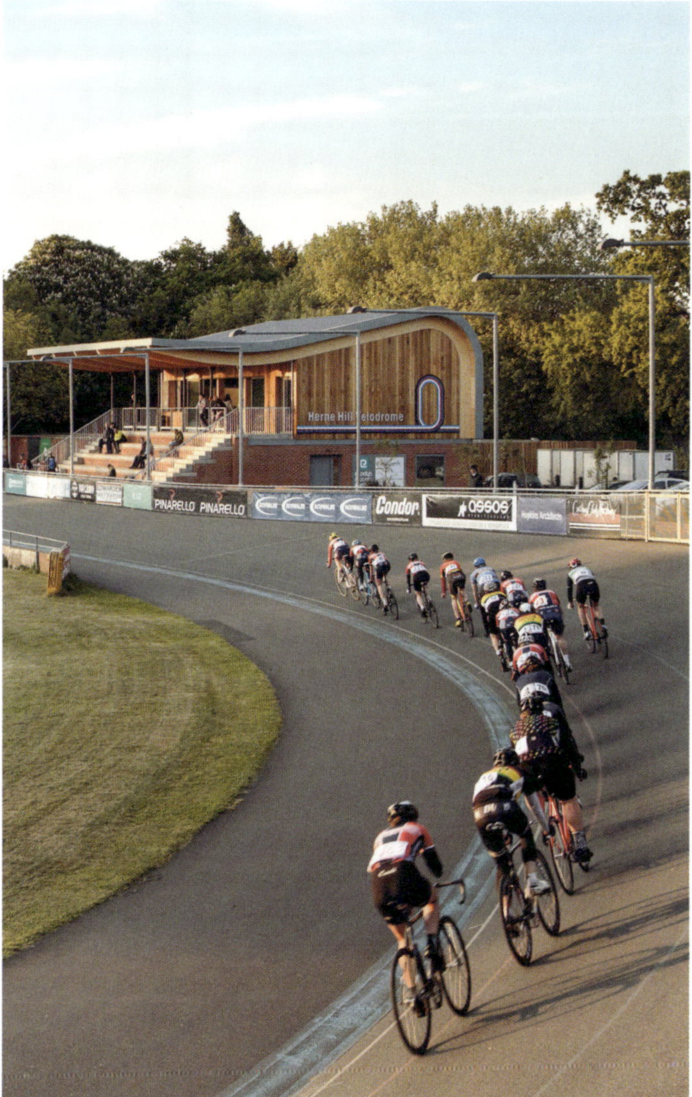

Herne Hill Velodrome
PINARELLO
PINARELLO
Condor
assos

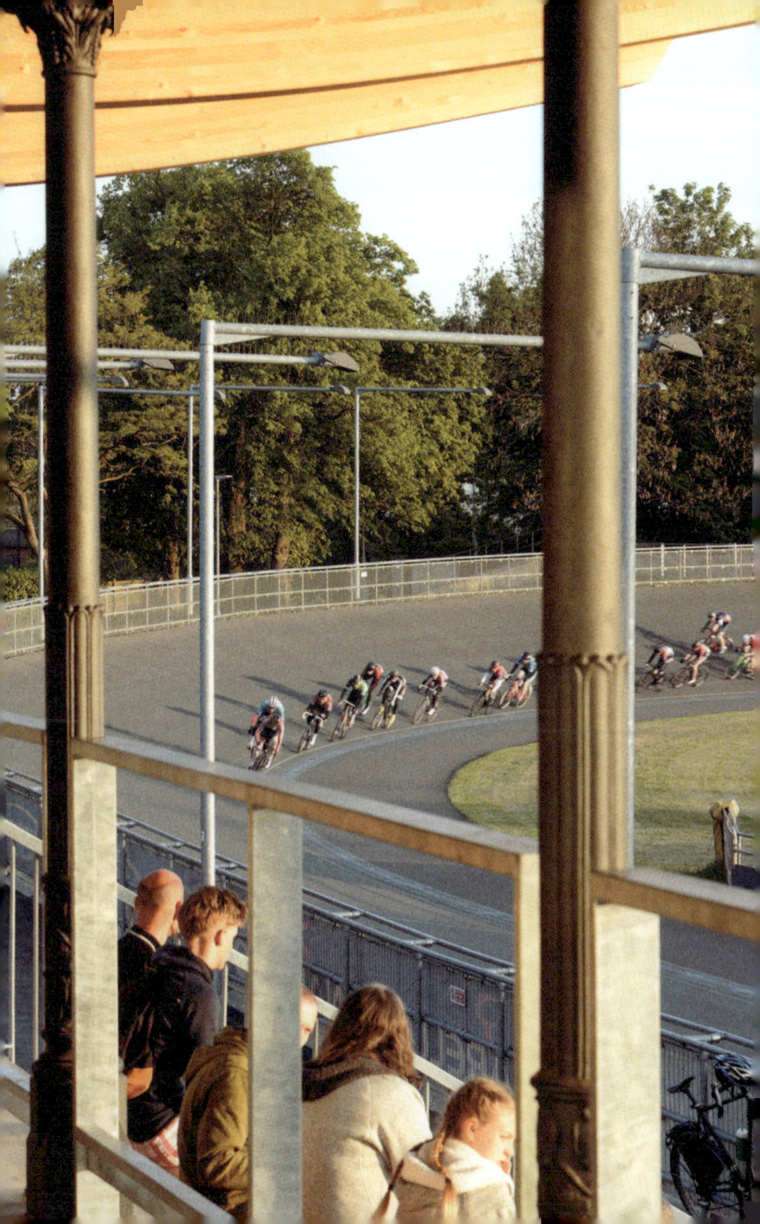

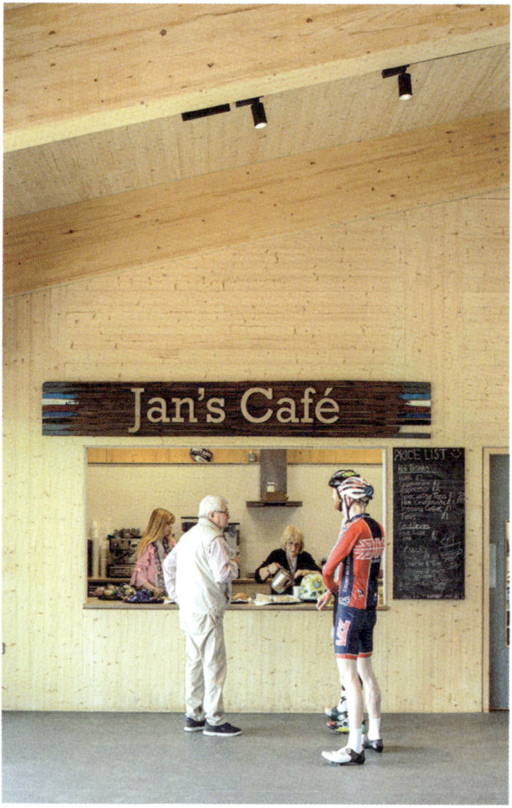
Jan's Café
PRICE LIST

21
BRIXTON CYCLES

Cooperatively-run south London institution

Racks of Brixton Cycle Club jerseys emblazoned in the Rastafarian colours of red, green, yellow and black pay tribute to the area's Caribbean heritage, which this place reps with pride. Founded in 1983, not long after the Brixton riots, Lambeth's much-loved worker-owned bike shop was the brainchild of two local friends who came up with the idea on a ride from Land's End to John O'Groats. Its staff – several of whom have worked here for decades – are among the most knowledgeable and committed in the capital, offering top-notch services and bespoke wheel builds alongside sales of Surly and Salsa frames, parts, accessories and some of the coolest merch in town.

296–298 Brixton Road, SW9 6AG
Nearest stations: Brixton, Stockwell
brixtoncycles.co.uk

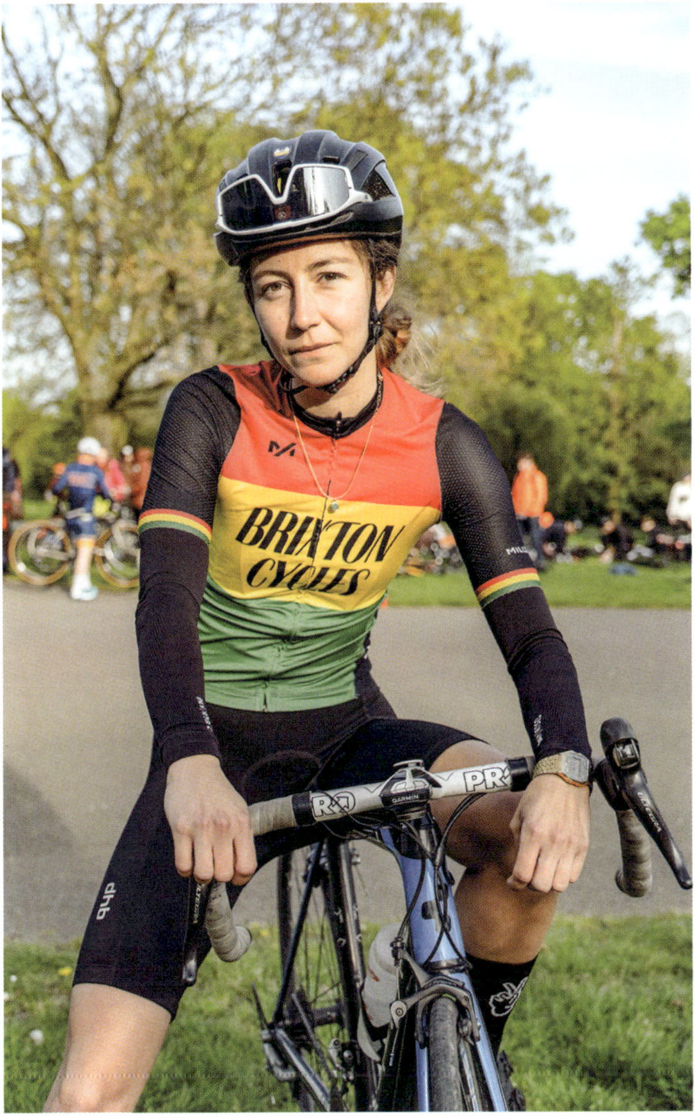
BRIXTON
CYCLES

22
GLORIA

Bespoke titanium specialists

If it's titanium you're after, you've come to the right place. Lighter than steel and even more luxurious to ride, titanium has a cult following. The only issue is that it is incredibly hard – quite literally – to put together and consequently comes at a cost. But this must-visit bike shop stocks those brands that have mastered the art while making them (somewhat) affordable: among others, they sell Genesis and J.Guillem, alongside Gloria's own make. They offer expert and attentive advice, and really take the time to explain things. If you decide that titanium is for you, it's worth getting insurance and a strong lock.

782 Fulham Road, SW6 5SL
Nearest station: Putney Bridge
gloriacycling.com

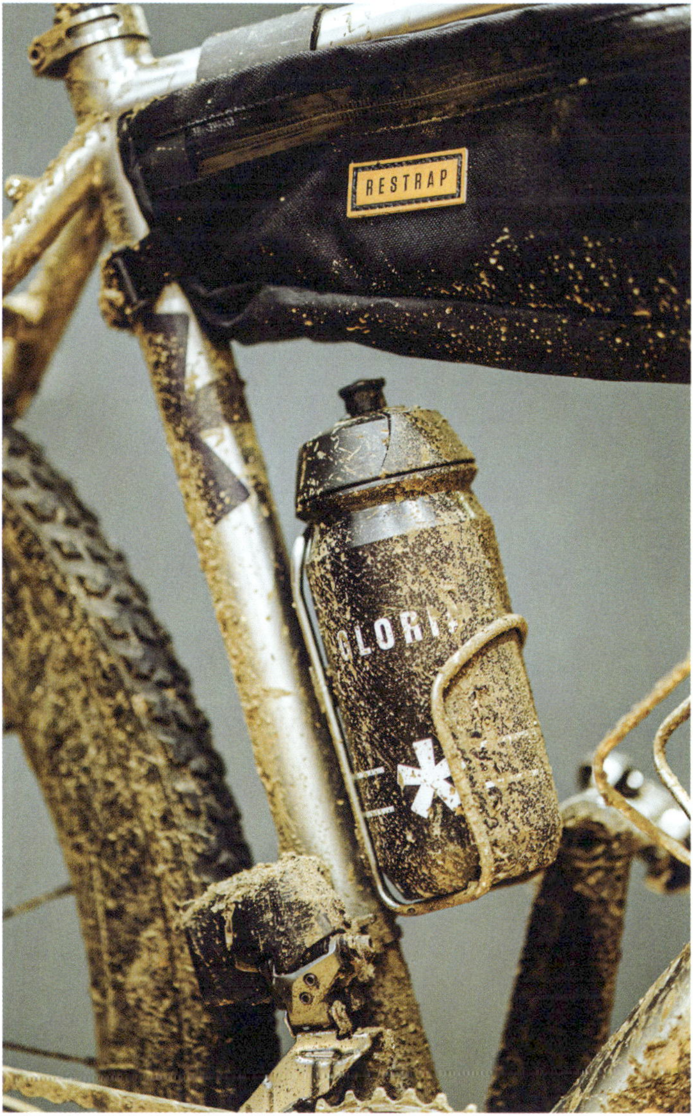
RESTRAP

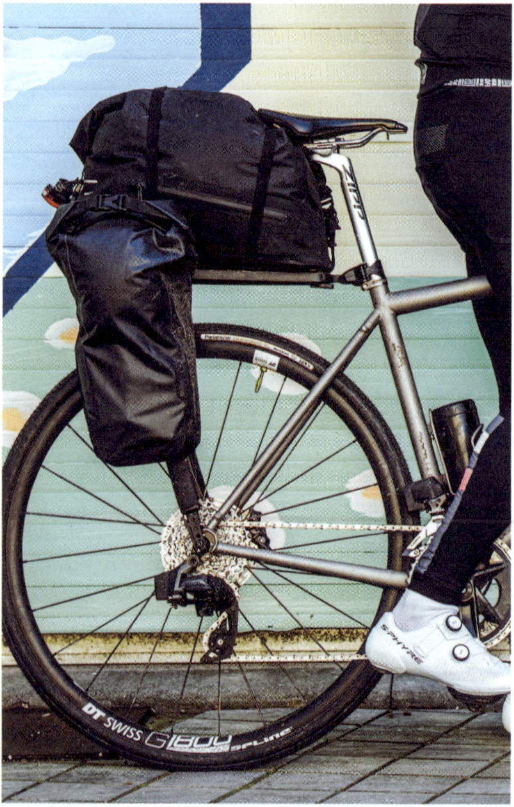
DT SWISS G1800 SPLINE
SPHYRE

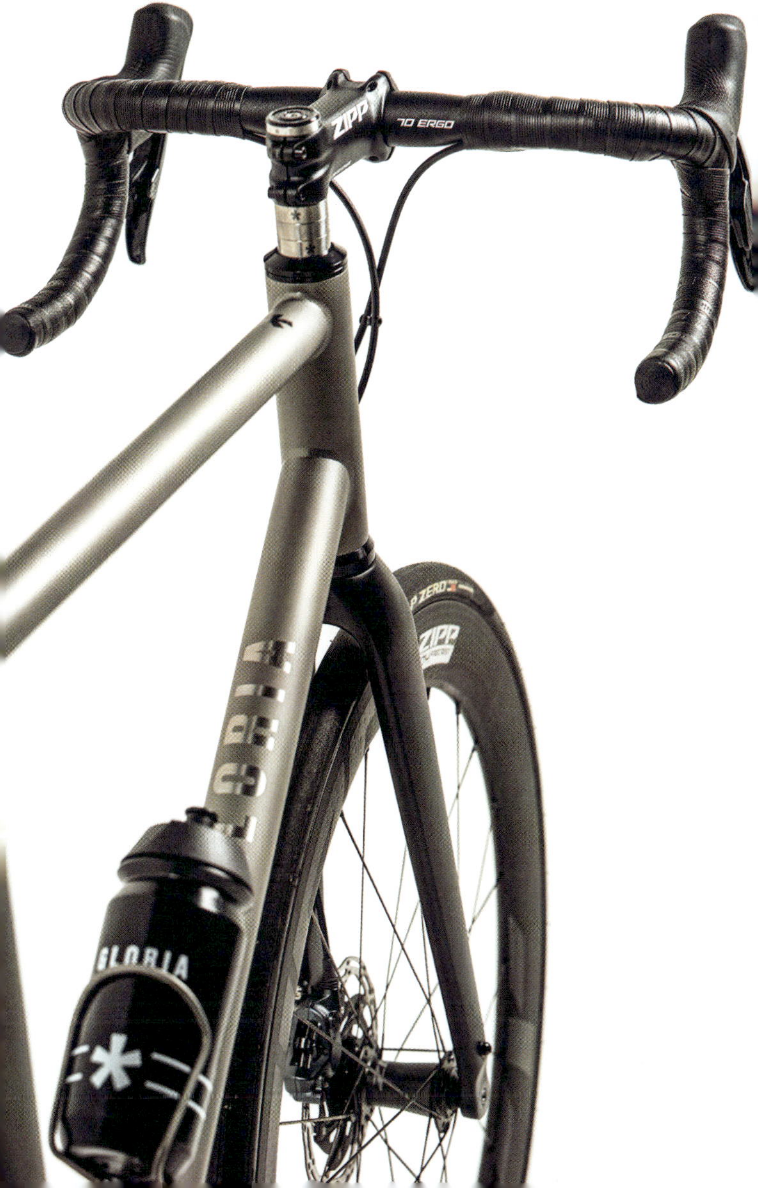
ZIPP
70 ERGO
GLORIA
ZIPP

23
XO BIKES

Refurbed bikes that help rebuild lives

Part of the joy of second-hand bikes is the stories they come with, and the bikes at XO have more history than most. Top brand bikes are donated – many by the Met Police unable to trace the original owners – and given TLC until they're as good as new. The mechanics doing them up are all prison leavers trained to a professional standard, and profit from sales goes back into the project. As well as the reasonably priced original finish bikes, XO offers special ranges with old branding painted over in XO's Swag Black and Hot Orange colours. Not looking for new wheels? Book your current frame in for a respray to get the look.

Unit 22/23, Lewisham Shopping Centre, SE13 7EP
Nearest station: Lewisham
Other location: Wandsworth
xobikes.com

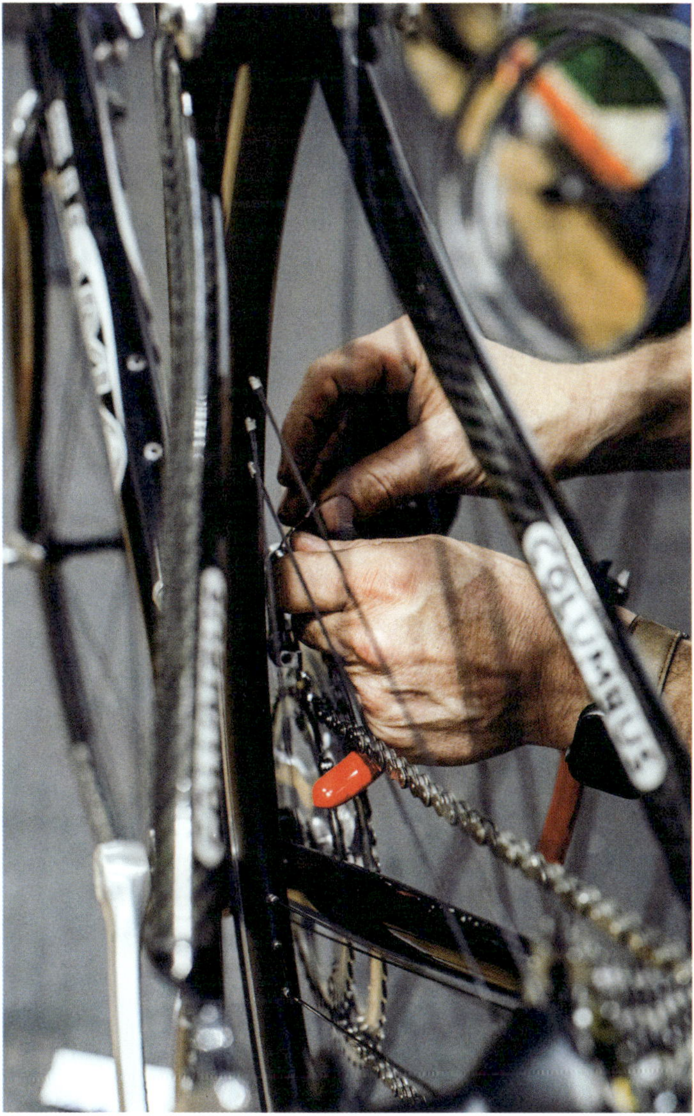
COLUMBUS

24

PEARSON

The world's oldest bike purveyor

Back in 1860, when this joint first opened its doors to customers, some Londoners were still getting around on penny-farthings. For better or worse, depending on your inclinations, you won't find any of those on sale here. Instead, the Sutton-based shop is bang up to date, offering stylish cycling garb and own-brand bikes. Pearson's first model was the Endeavour and today their bikes ship globally. If you swing by in person you can get a precision custom bike fitting and pick up some new Lycra while you're at it. The enduring popularity of Pearson is proof of this family business's knack for moving with the times. Long may it continue.

232 Upper Richmond Road, SW14 8AG
Nearest station: Mortlake
pearson1860.com

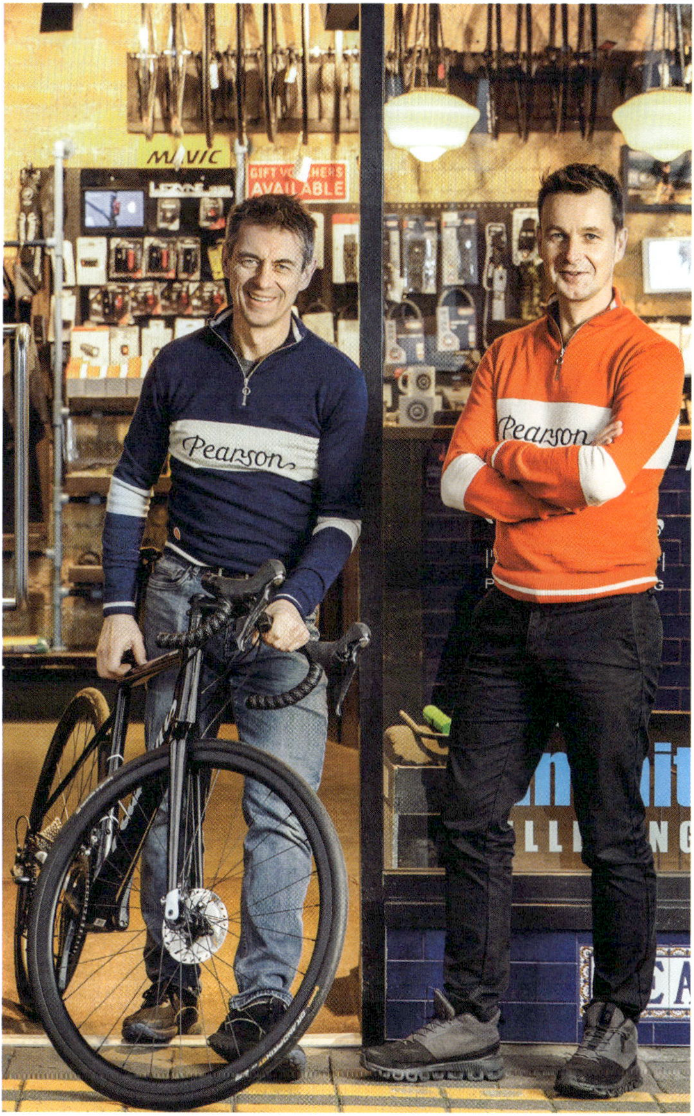
MAVIC
AVAILABLE
Pearson
Pearson

25
FULLY CHARGED

Riding the crest of London's e-bike wave

A bike is so much more than wheels, frame, saddle, pedals and some handlebars. A bike is freedom. The freedom to go where you want, when you want. E-bikes take this one step further, bringing the liberating power of cycling to even more people – those who might find pedalling a standard bike difficult, have kids to transport or businesses wanting to avoid congestion and minimise their carbon tyre print. E-bikes are the future of urban mobility. In London – and beyond – Fully Charged are powering ahead, leading the vanguard of an unstoppable electric evolution.

Arch 6, Unit 5, Crucifix Lane, SE1 3JW
Nearest station: London Bridge
fullycharged.com

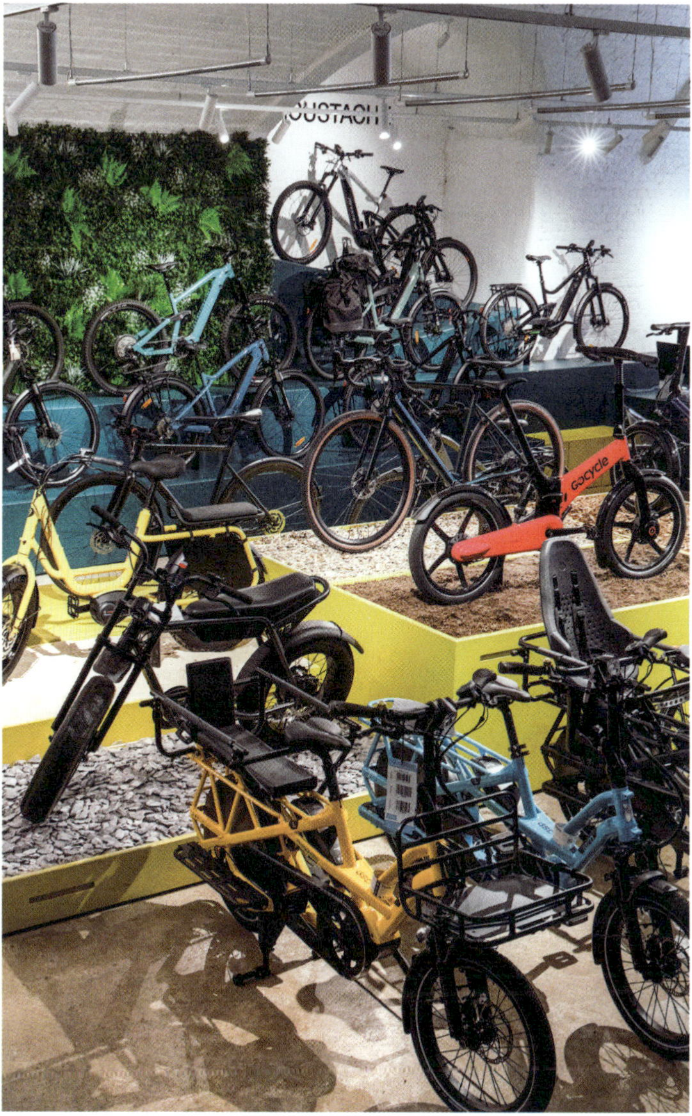
Gocycle

26
SEABASS CYCLES

Indie store keeping community alive

Seabass Cycles knows how to have fun. To celebrate its tenth birthday in 2023, the team threw a banging party with live bands at their regular under-the-arches haunt, Moor Beer Vaults. To this gang, cycling isn't a lone sport; it's social. Tag along on a 'shop ride' around the city, topped off with pizza and pints, or pitch in on a weekend wild camping trip headed out of London. You'll find yourself welcomed into an instant bike crew. The shop specialises in customising Brother, Cannondale, Genesis, Ritchey and Surly frames, selling accessories and offering bike fittings, repairs and services.

261 Rye Lane, SE15 4UR
Nearest station: Peckham Rye
seabasscycles.co.uk

Pasela
700 x

Vittoria
Randonneur
700 x 28

27

RAPHA LONDON CLUBHOUSE

Stylish cycle wear for aficionados

Rapha will go down in history as the brand that made Lycra hip. Set up in 2004 by a pair of bike evangelists with a background in branding, the company has become a global sensation, with Rapha Cycling Club 'chapters' around the world and sponsorship for Tour de France champions Team Sky and Team Wiggins. The Soho base is a hub where you can catch talks and exhibitions, hire a bike or kick back in the cafe and refuel on antipasti while watching the Giro d'Italia. The design-led apparel comes with a hefty price tag, but the quality and customer service are impeccable. Love them or loathe them, they've achieved something extraordinary in reshaping the aesthetics of cycling.

85 Brewer Street, W1F 9ZN
Nearest station: Piccadilly Circus
rapha.cc/gb/en/clubhouses/london

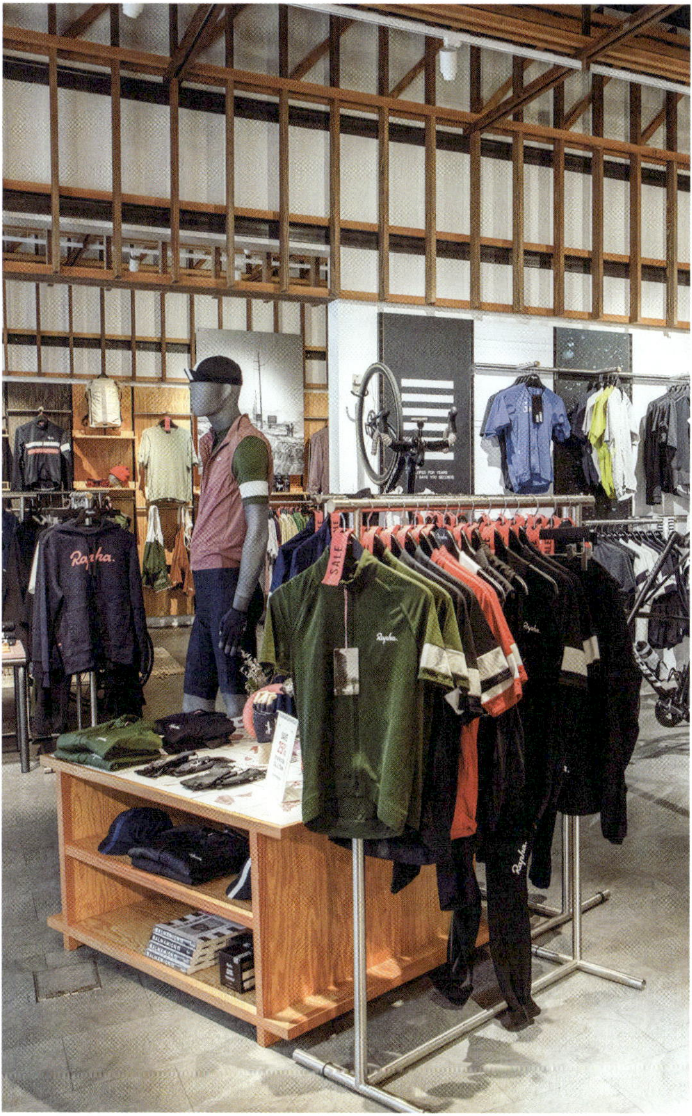
Rapha.
SALE

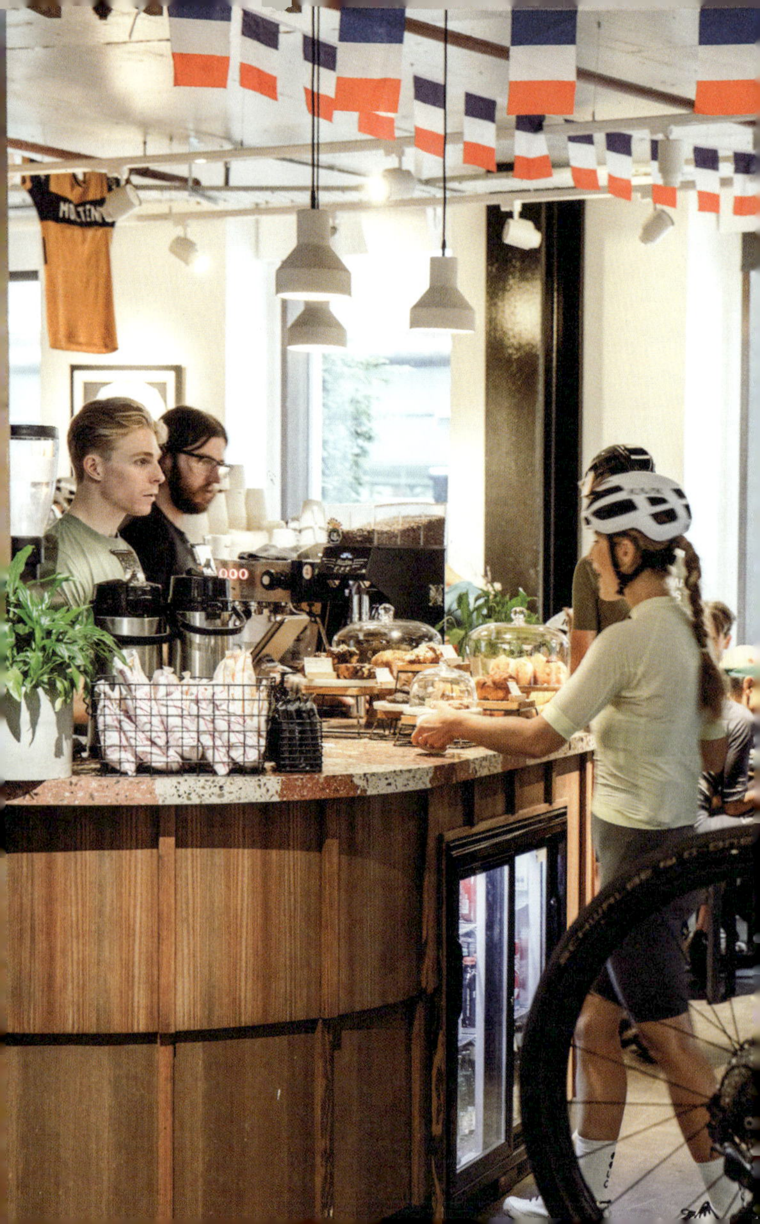

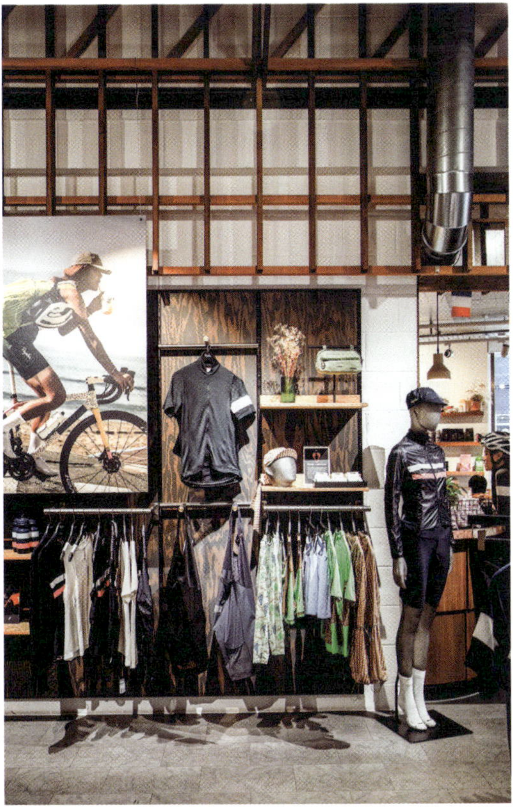

28
SIGMA SPORTS

Cycle shop with online treasure

If you're looking to buy anything cycling-related online, Sigma Sports has by far the superior selection. So much so that it's hard to believe the founders started it as a passion project flogging bikes from one of their bedrooms. At their flagship store you can peruse the wonderful range of road, mountain, gravel, hybrid, cargo, folding and e-bikes, and get a service or a bike fitting. Since 1992, Sigma has been embedded in the cycling community, supporting legends like Tim Don, Bradley Wiggins and Ryan Mullen, but it's also the retailer of choice for cyclists of all abilities, with premium wares sold by a welcoming, knowledgeable team. While some in the trade are sadly shutting, Sigma has expanded, opening branches in the Midlands and Surrey.

St Johns Place, 37–43 High Street, KT1 4DA
Nearest station: Hampton Wick
sigmasports.com

SIGMA
SPORTS
cape the elements
Embrace the elements
Don't let the weather interrupt your training this season

29
PEDAL BACK CYCLING

Cycle cafe big on camaraderie

What's not to love about toasties named after your cycling heroines? Tuck into the Atherton, the Kadeena or the Archibald. Pedal Back can't promise their sarnies will give you talent on the track but, with Putney Bakehouse sourdough and tasty fillings, they are certainly worth the visit anyway. The cafe/shop/workshop started life in Tooting's Broadway Market but has been based in Fulham since 2019, stocking everything from Quella bikes to bells and lights, locks and 'Afro pop' socks. Pedal Back's cycling club is the least cliquey in town; with a firm no-judgement policy on what type of bike you ride and encouragement to go at your own pace, it's perfect for newbies.

24 Lillie Road, SW6 1TS
Nearest station: West Brompton
pedalbackcycling.com

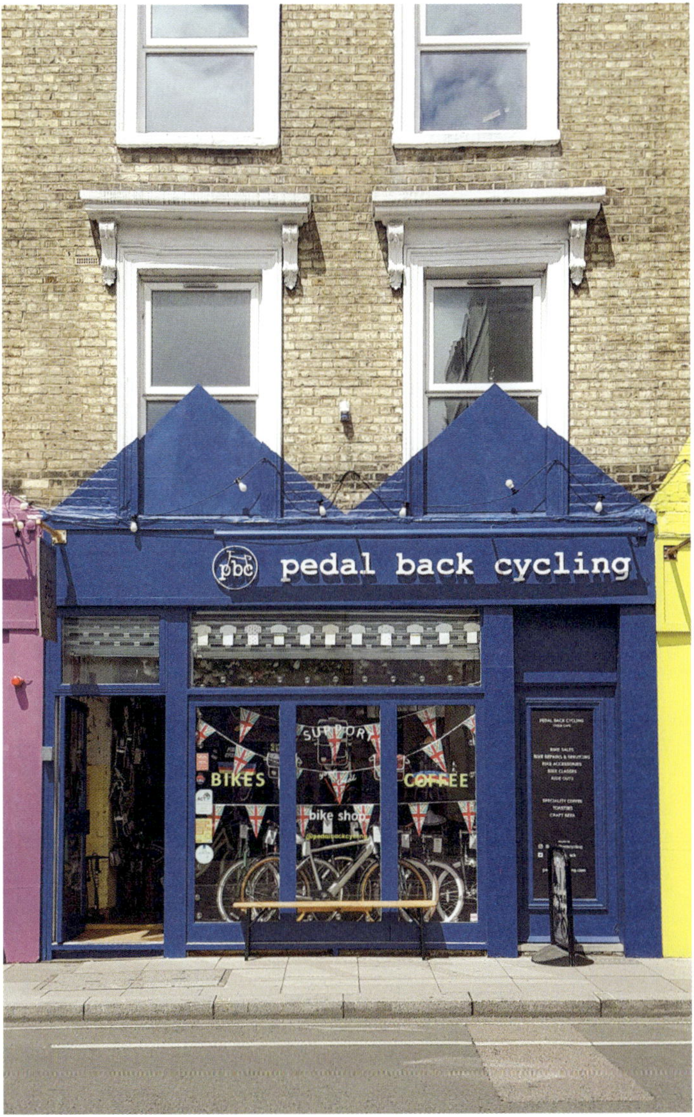
pbc
pedal back cycling
SUPPORT
BIKES
COFFEE
bike shop

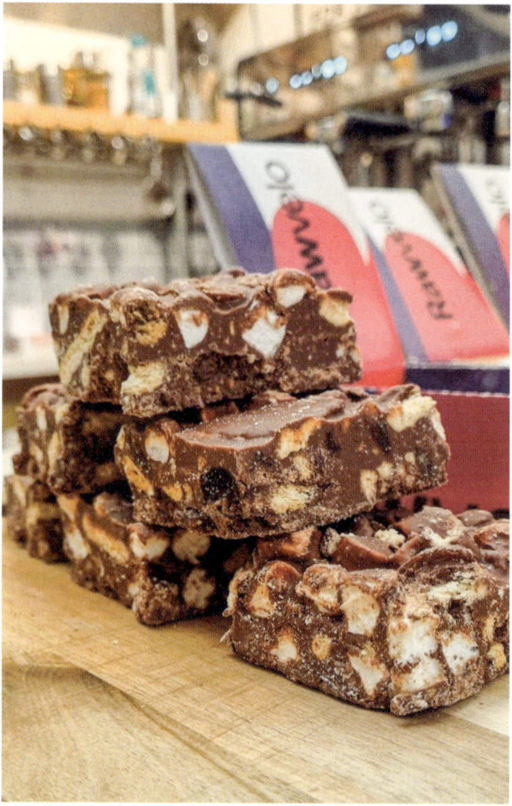

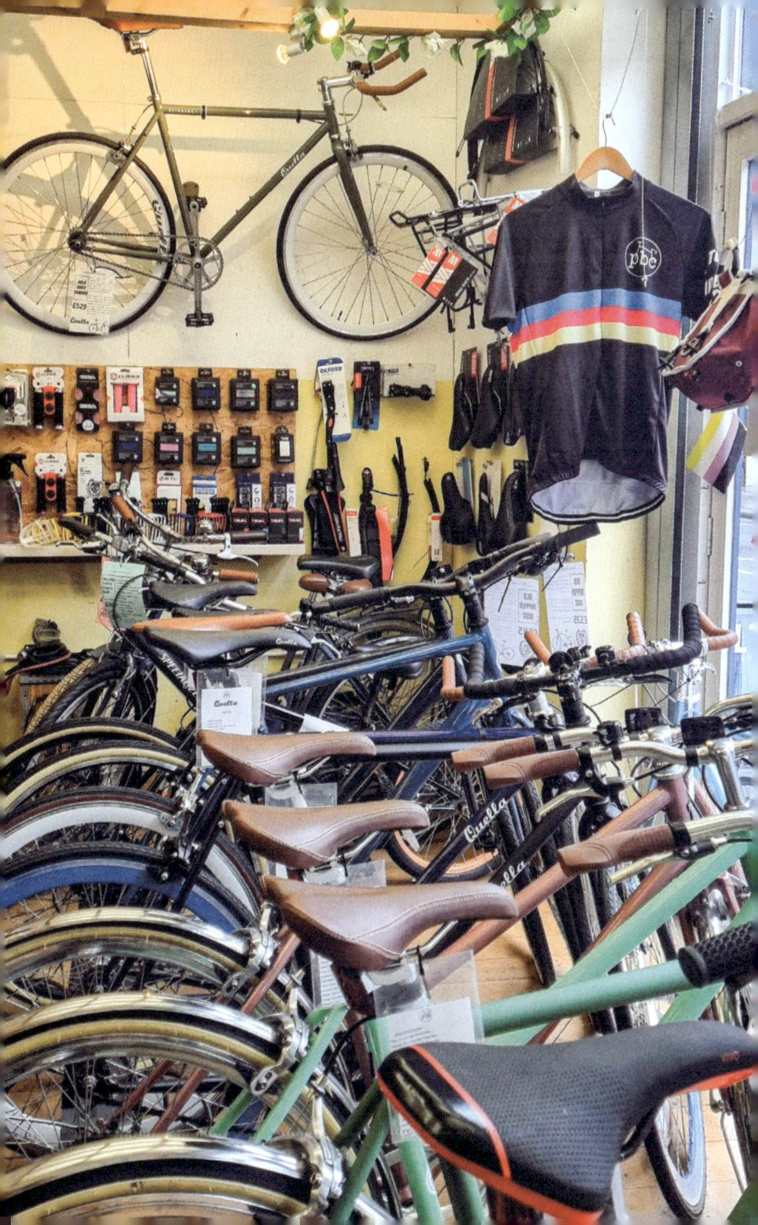

Quella
£529
OXFORD
pbc
Quella
Quella

30
FAIRLIGHT CYCLES

World-leading bikes with rave reviews

Dom Thomas, the man behind Fairlight, is a uniquely talented designer. There's nothing he hasn't considered in conceptualising what a utility, all-season or cross-country bike could be. Frames are manufactured abroad in Taiwan, tubes are supplied by Reynolds (resident in Birmingham) and the bikes are put together in London and imbued with a certain cycling magic. Smart, comfortable and superbly capable, these steel beauties are a particular favourite with the bike-packing crowd. And the pundits can't get enough of them, consistently giving them 5 stars in the cycling press (where normally 4 stars are reserved for the very best). Take one for a spin and you'll soon discover why.

Florentia Clothing Village, Haringey, N4 1TD
(By appointment only)
Nearest stations: Stamford Hill, Manor House
fairlightcycles.com

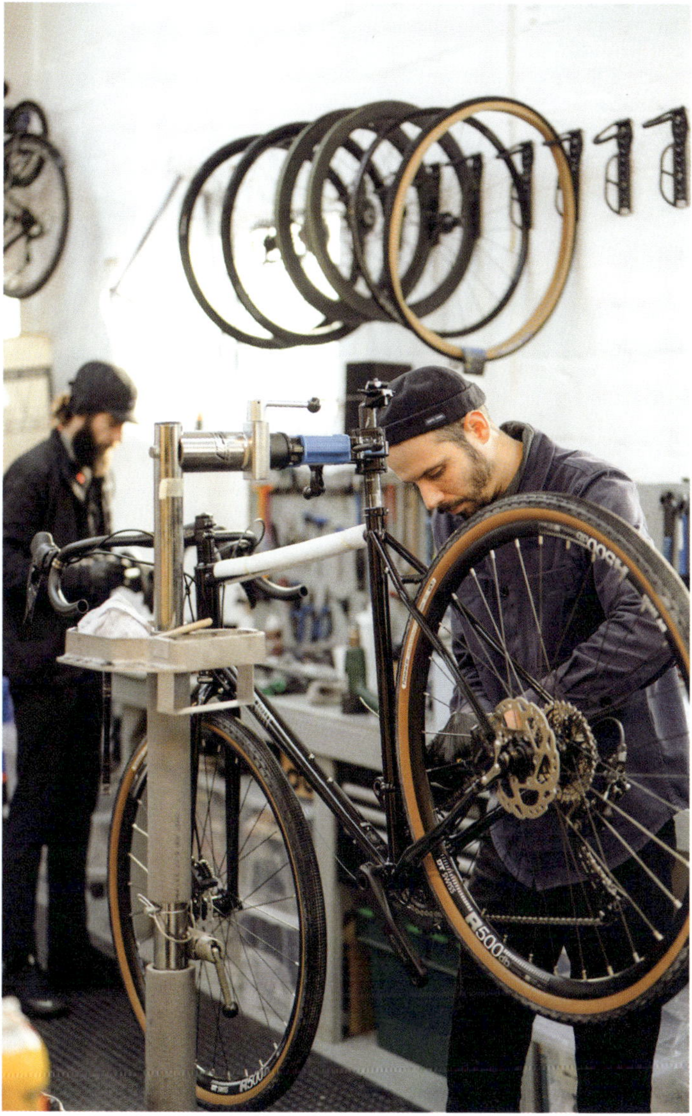
R500

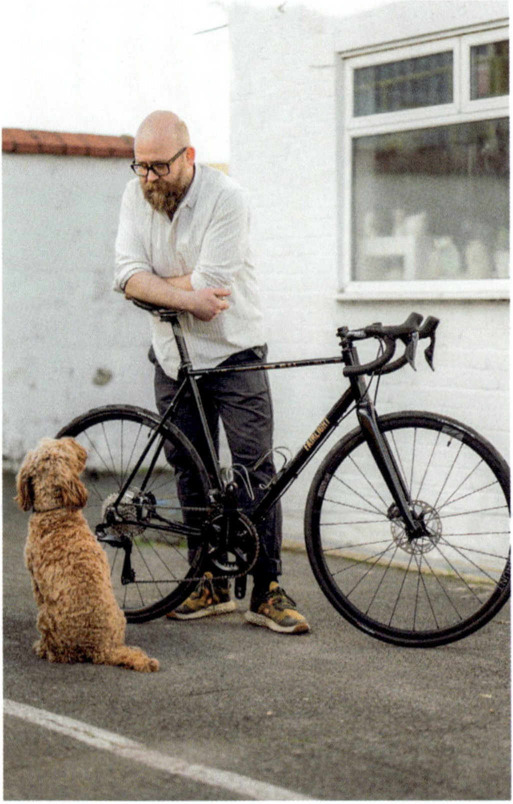

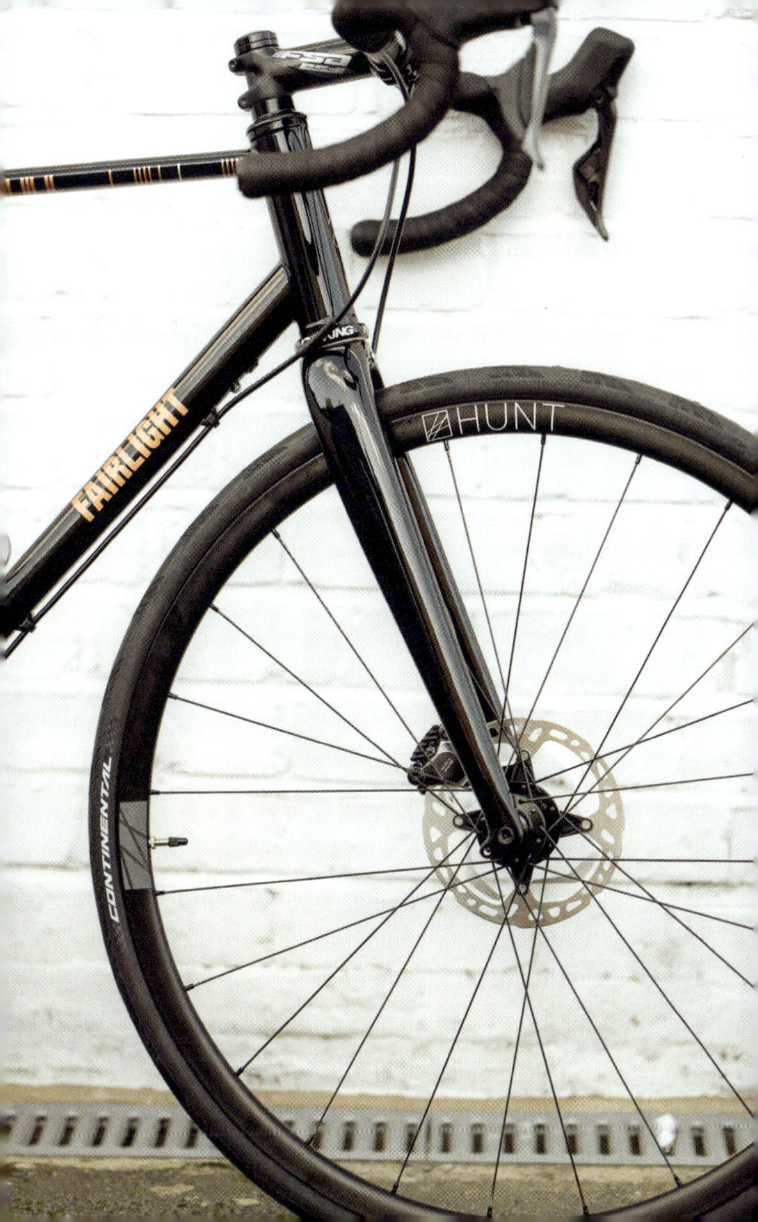

FAIRLIGHT
HUNT
CONTINENTAL

THE HACKNEY PEDDLER

Vintage specialists with a cult following

Going into the Hackney Peddler is like stepping back in time. The shop is filled with lovingly restored steel bikes from – depending on your age – your teens, childhood or the retro movies you watch as an adult. Raleigh, Peugeot, Eddy Merckx and Colnago frames from the 1970–90s are found at every turn and in every hue imaginable, available to buy off the shelf or order bespoke. Not only are the bikes heart-stoppingly beautiful and made to last, but punters also rave about the service, with friendly staff who go above and beyond to make sure you and your new steed are perfectly matched. Say hello to Monty, the shop's charming dog-in-residence, who you'll find lounging by the window.

89 Stoke Newington Road, N16 8AA
Nearest stations: Rectory Road, Dalston Kingsland
thehackneypeddler.co.uk

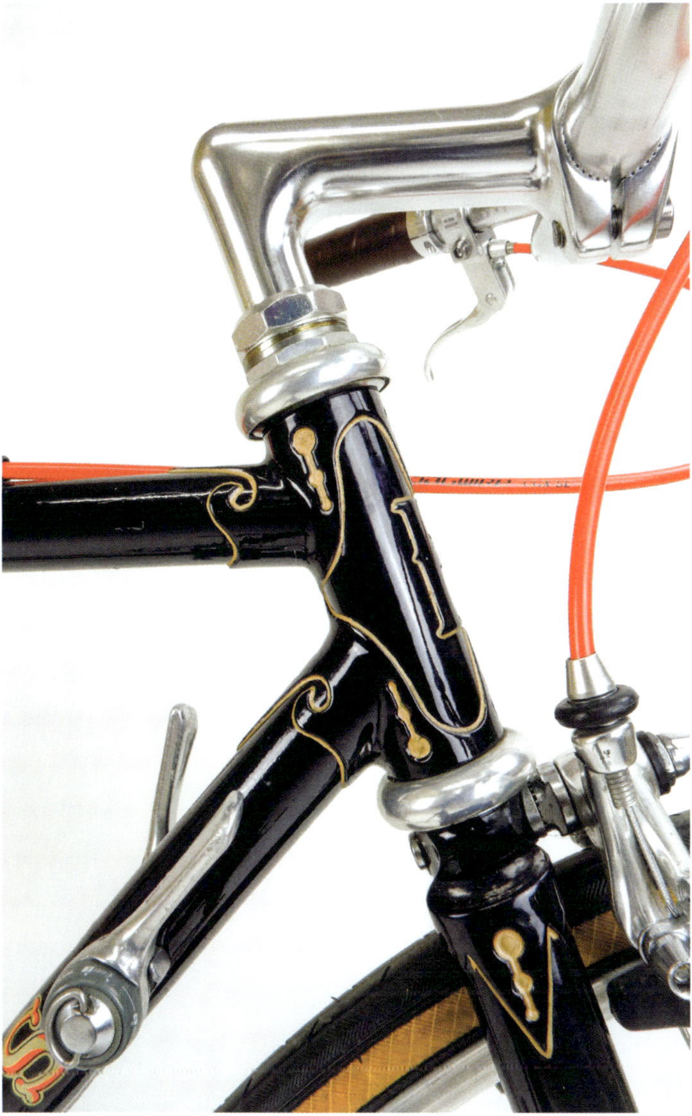

32
VIA ATELIER

It's not just a shop, it's an atelier

This ultra-chic King's Cross hotspot is located in a former grain store within the achingly elegant Coal Drops Yard. Everything is super high-end, design-led and aesthetically just so, from custom builds by Pegoretti and Passoni to the seasonal craft coffee served at the VIA cafe. It's drenched in cycling's European heritage and is the destination du jour for the image-conscious bike geeks among us with cash to spare. And though it kind of makes us hate ourselves to admit it, we can't get enough of this place. It absolutely takes the yellow jersey. Just bury your credit card in your deepest saddlebag.

18-19 Stable Street, N1C 4AB
Nearest station: Kings Cross
via-atelier.cc

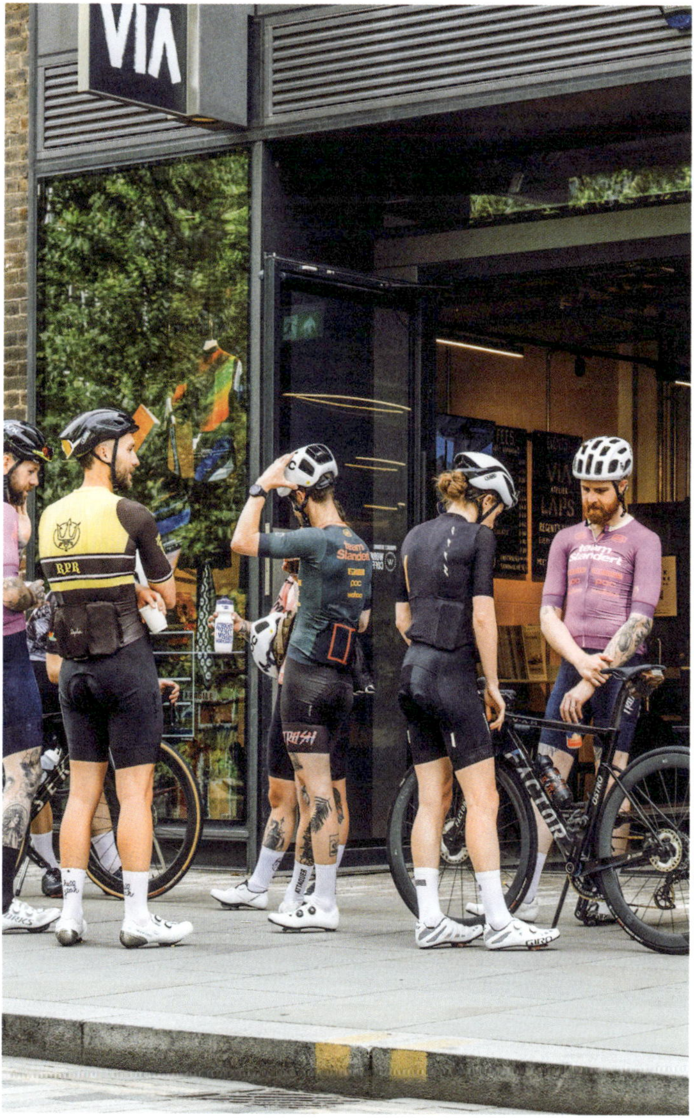
VIA
RPR
team Standert
team Standert
FACTOR

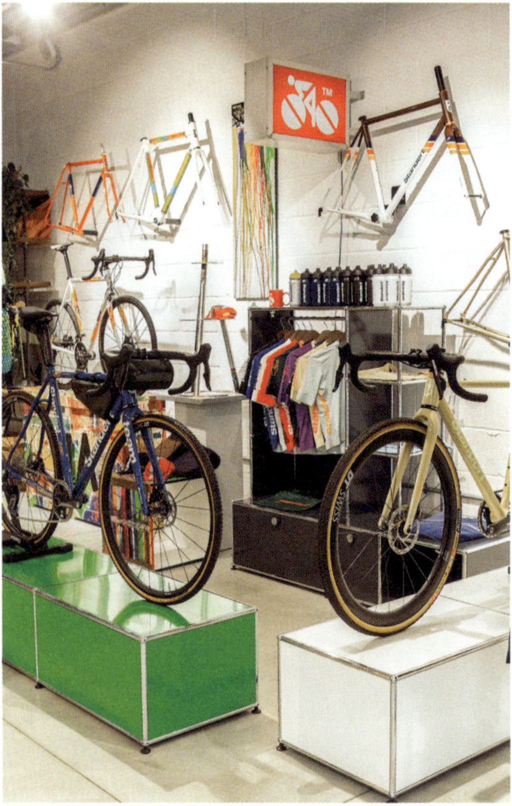

PAS NORMAL
STUDIOS
INTERNATIONAL CYCLING CLUB

33
PAUL SMITH

Dapper designer cycling apparel

In another life, Paul Smith would have been a professional cyclist. Growing up in Nottingham, bikes were his passion and he was talented too, hitting record times on the track. But he was forced to switch gear after a crash hospitalised him for months. Throughout his career in design, his love of cycling has remained steadfast and he fuses the two in his stylish bike gear and accessories, including colourful bib shorts, Allen key sets, socks and helmets. Smith is obsessed with cycling's 1950–60s heyday, citing Jacques Anquetil as his all-time hero, and has teamed up with Rapha to produce a range of retro clothing inspired by the infinitely chic French and Italian cyclists of the past.

57-58 Coal Drops Yard, N1C 4DQ
Nearest station: Kings Cross
paulsmith.com/uk

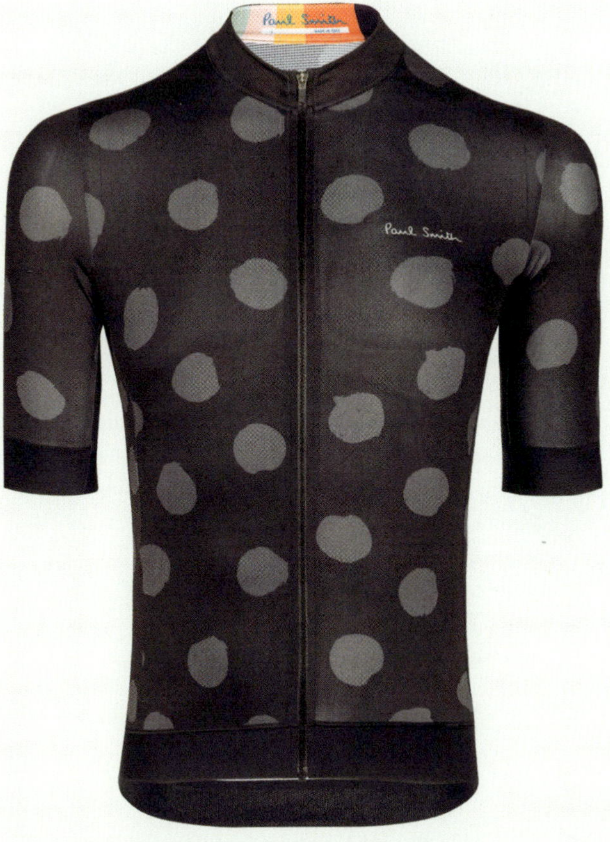
Paul Smith
Paul Smith

34

LONDON GREEN CYCLES

London's original cargo bike specialists

The Christiania cargo bike was created in Freetown Christiania, a counter-cultural neighbourhood in Copenhagen where cars are banned. The wooden box-fronted bike was invented as a solution to carting around food, firewood and children. London isn't yet a motor-free utopia, but utility bikes are soaring in popularity. London Green Cycles is the only official Christiania vendor in the capital, also selling Yuba, Bicicapace, Bakfiets and Babboe models, kids' bikes and a colourful range of accessories. They offer test rides and longer hires as well as repairing cargo bikes – which few mechanics do. They also rent to businesses and television companies. So if you spot a cargo bike in *Motherland* or *Midsomer Murders*, it's from here.

4 Chester Court, Albany Street, NW1 4BU
Nearest stations: Great Portland Street, Euston
londongreencycles.co.uk

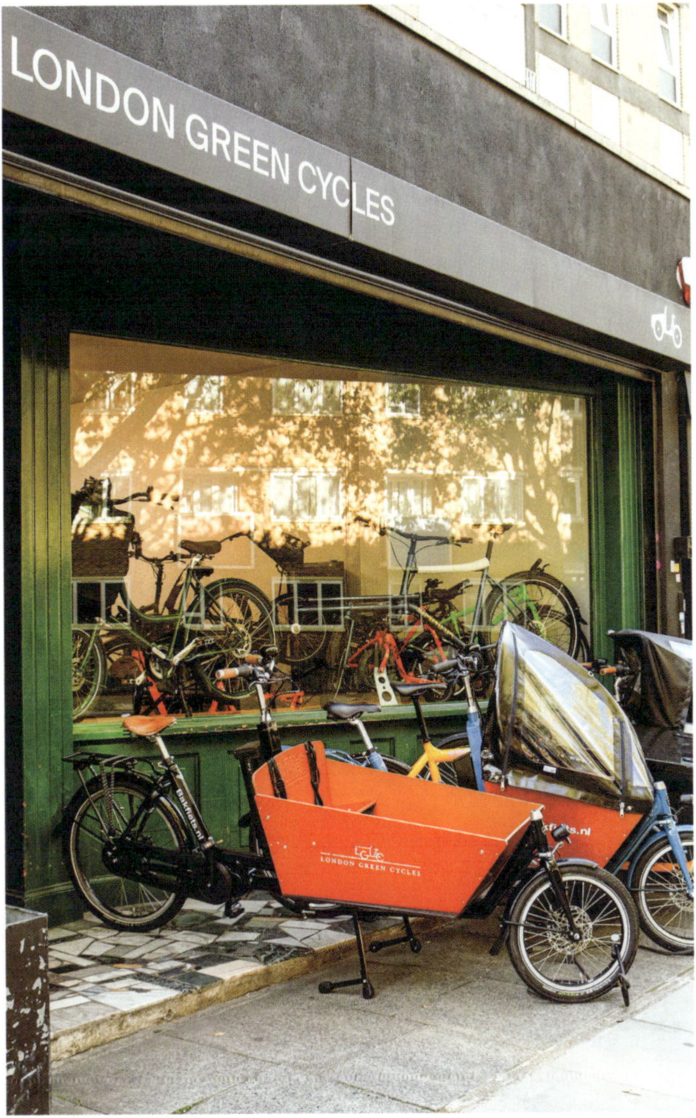
LONDON GREEN CYCLES
Bakfiets.nl
LONDON GREEN CYCLES

35

THE SPOKE

Local bike-friendly pit stop

We cyclists have a long-standing love affair with coffee. Caffeine can give us the edge as we set off in the saddle or provide a much-needed restorative at the end of a long ride. Grabbing a double espresso at The Spoke, you might find yourself surrounded by friendly faces from Islington Cycling Club, as this is the end-point on one of the north London club's routes. The cafe's owners are big into cycling and it shows in the decor – a wheel on the exterior, pannier racks adorning the walls. It's a good feeling to be in a spot run by people who love cycling as much as you do (and the coffee goes down a treat, too).

710 Holloway Road, N19 3NH
Nearest stations: Upper Holloway, Archway
thespokelondon.com

the SPOKE
the SPOKE
EST·2014
WINE &
COCKTAILS
BURGERS
& BEER
COCKTAILS
WINE
BEER
and
AMAZING
BURGERS

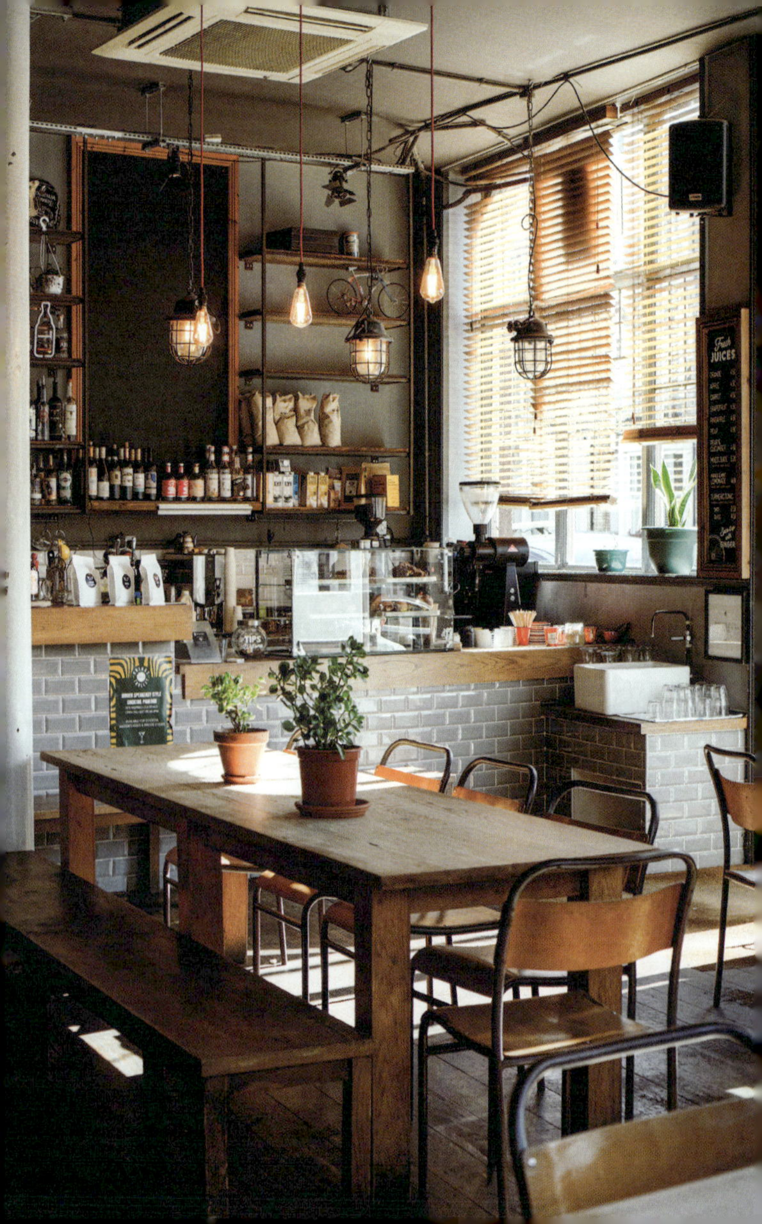
Fresh JUICES
TIPS

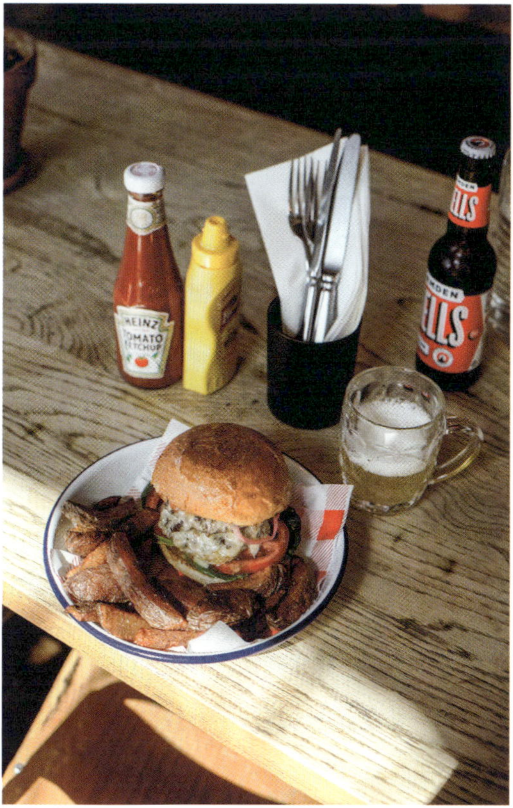
HEINZ
TOMATO
KETCHUP

36
URBAN HILL CLIMB

Test your endurance or enjoy the spectacle

Welcome to Swain's Lane, host to London's most iconic and brutal hill climb where the steepest gradients hit 20 per cent. Cyclists train here all year but, on one day in autumn, it becomes a festival of fun and suffering. For the hardcore, this is a race to the top, but there's a cheerful contingent of participants in fancy dress too, blasting out tunes through speakers. For friends and fans, it's an amusing day out in leafy Highgate. Crowds cheer from the side-lines, gawping at the assortment of agonised expressions as cyclists tackle the 900-metre stretch. However you choose to experience it, this event should be in every London cyclist's calendar.

Swain's Lane, N6
Nearest station: Archway
lcc.org.uk/events/urban-hill-climb-2023

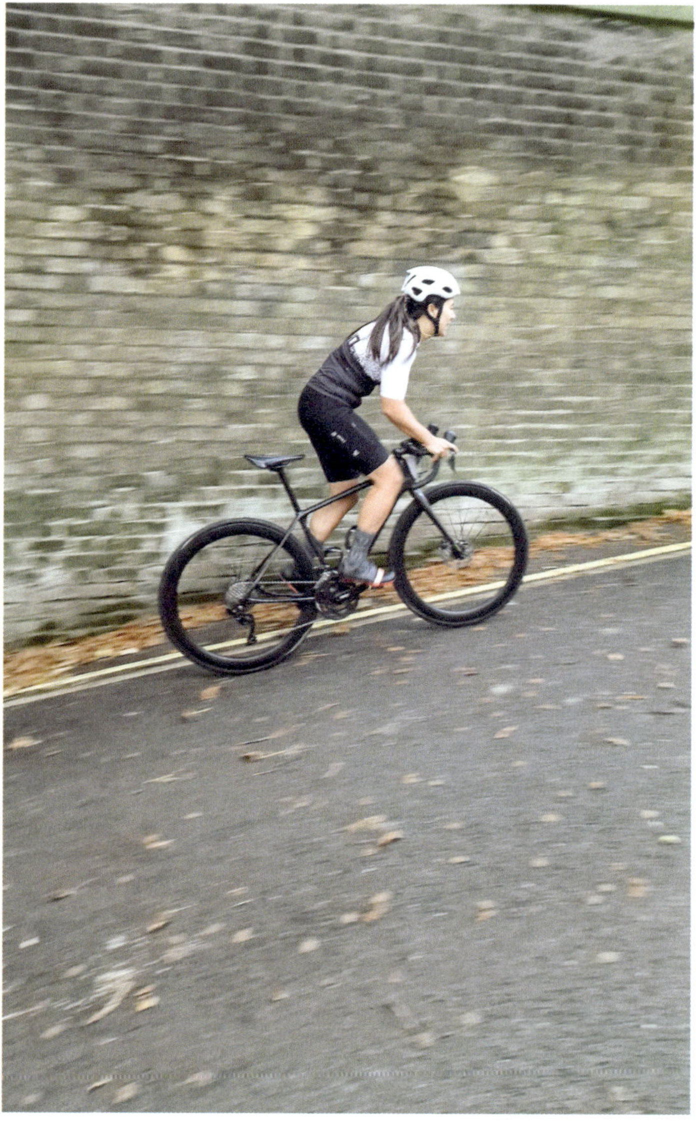

THE BEST RIDES IN AND AROUND LONDON

Here are some brilliant rides which will appeal to both those looking for something gentle and those looking to really stretch their legs. Compiled with special thanks to Andy Donohoe at Hub Vélo (no. 8).

RIDE 1: Sightseeing From the Saddle	9km / 20–35 minutes
RIDE 2: Regent's Park Laps	5km / 10–20 minutes
RIDE 3: Tour de Richmond Park	10km / 25–45 minutes
RIDE 4: Grand Union Canal	6km / 20–35 minutes
RIDE 5: Thames Path, Out East	30km / 1.5–2 hours
RIDE 6: Up the Lea Valley	54km / 2–3.5 hours
RIDE 7: Beyond Epping Forest	104km / 4–7 hours
RIDE 8: The Surrey Hills	85km / 3.5–5.5 hours
RIDE 9: The Kent Hills	75km / 3–5 hours
RIDE 10: Escape to the Chilterns	128km / 5–8.5 hours
RIDE 11: Winding Lanes of Hertfordshire	79km / 3–5.5 hours
RIDE 12: The Ultimate London-Brighton	95km / 4–6.5 hours

London Area Map

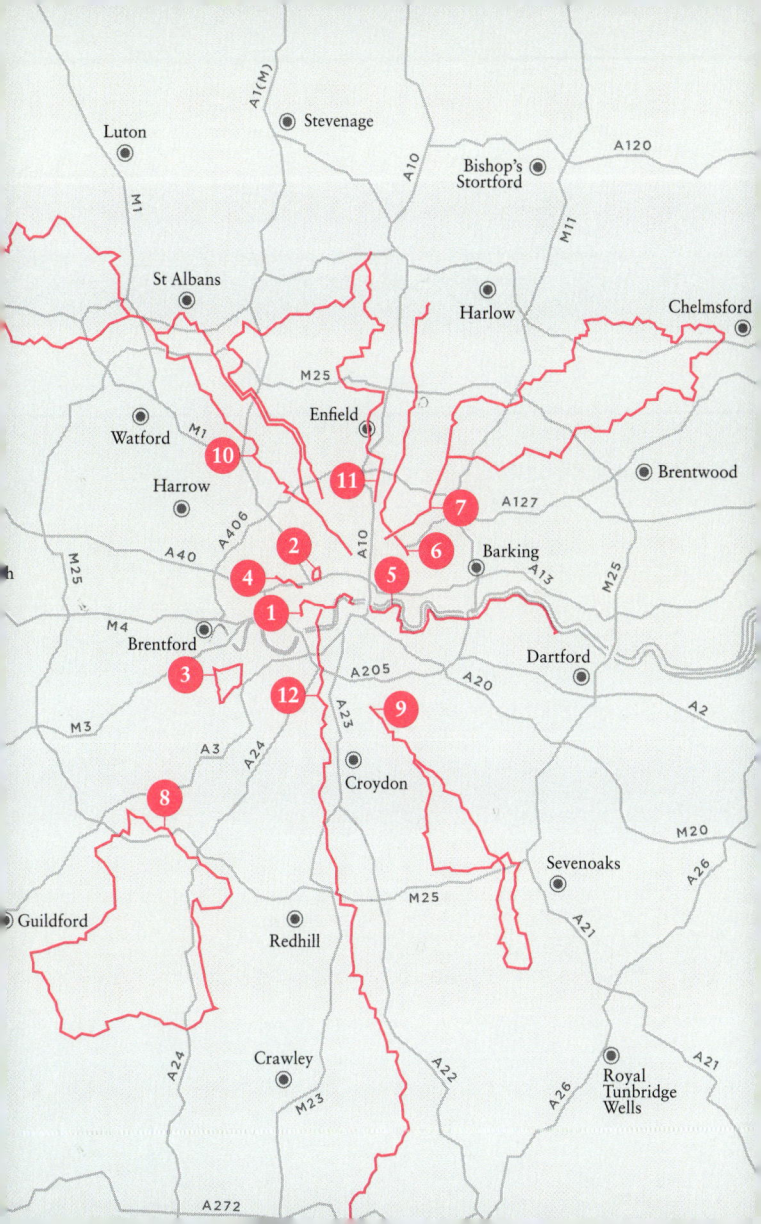

- Luton
- Stevenage
- St Albans
- Bishop's Stortford
- Chelmsford
- Harlow
- Watford
- Harrow
- Enfield
- Brentwood
- Brentford
- Barking
- Dartford
- Guildford
- Croydon
- Sevenoaks
- Redhill
- Crawley
- Royal Tunbridge Wells

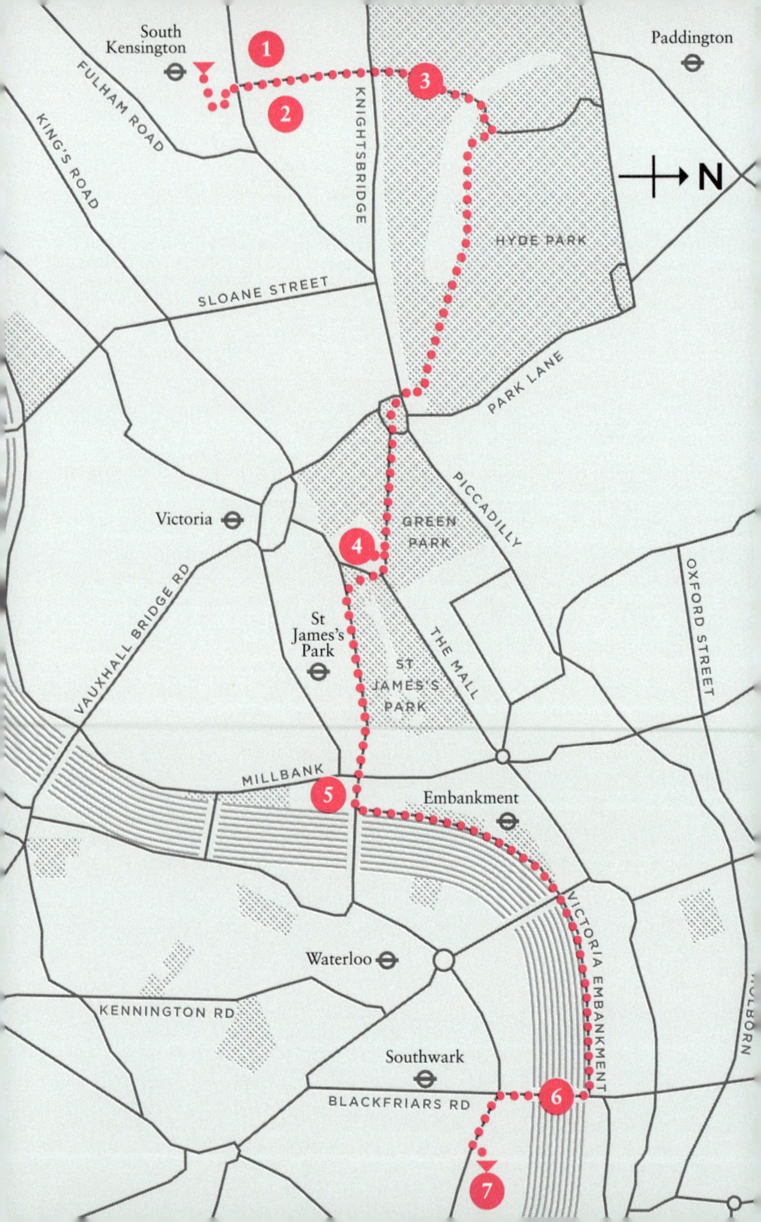
South Kensington
1
2
3
FULHAM ROAD
KING'S ROAD
KNIGHTSBRIDGE
Paddington
N
HYDE PARK
SLOANE STREET
PARK LANE
PICCADILLY
Victoria
GREEN PARK
4
St James's Park
ST JAMES'S PARK
THE MALL
VAUXHALL BRIDGE RD
OXFORD STREET
MILLBANK
5
Embankment
VICTORIA EMBANKMENT
Waterloo
KENNINGTON RD
Southwark
BLACKFRIARS RD
6
7

RIDE 1

SIGHTSEEING FROM THE SADDLE

Distance: 9km / 5.5 miles
Riding time (w/o stops): 20–35 minutes
Difficulty: Flat and easy to navigate but avoid rush hour

This winding road through central London begins in South Kensington: glide past the Natural History Museum ❶ and Victoria & Albert ❷ before cycling through Kensington Gardens and the verdant Hyde Park ❸. You'll have to weave around the tourists gathering outside Buckingham Palace ❹ before reaching the Houses of Parliament ❺. Make your way along the Thames and watch out for the rising skyline of glass and steel as you head east, past the London Eye, before finally crossing Tower Bridge ❻ and into Borough Market ❼, where much-deserved lunch awaits.

To see the full route scan the QR code or go to:
hoxtonminipress.com/pages/ride1

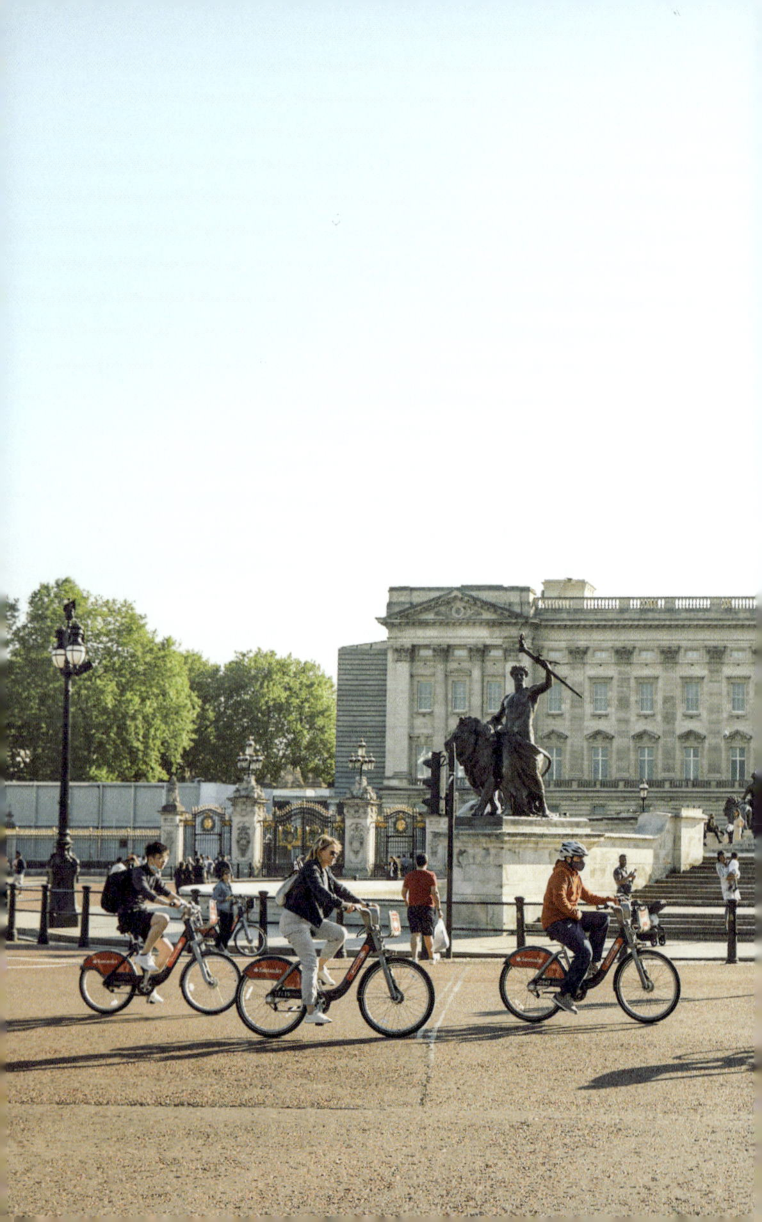

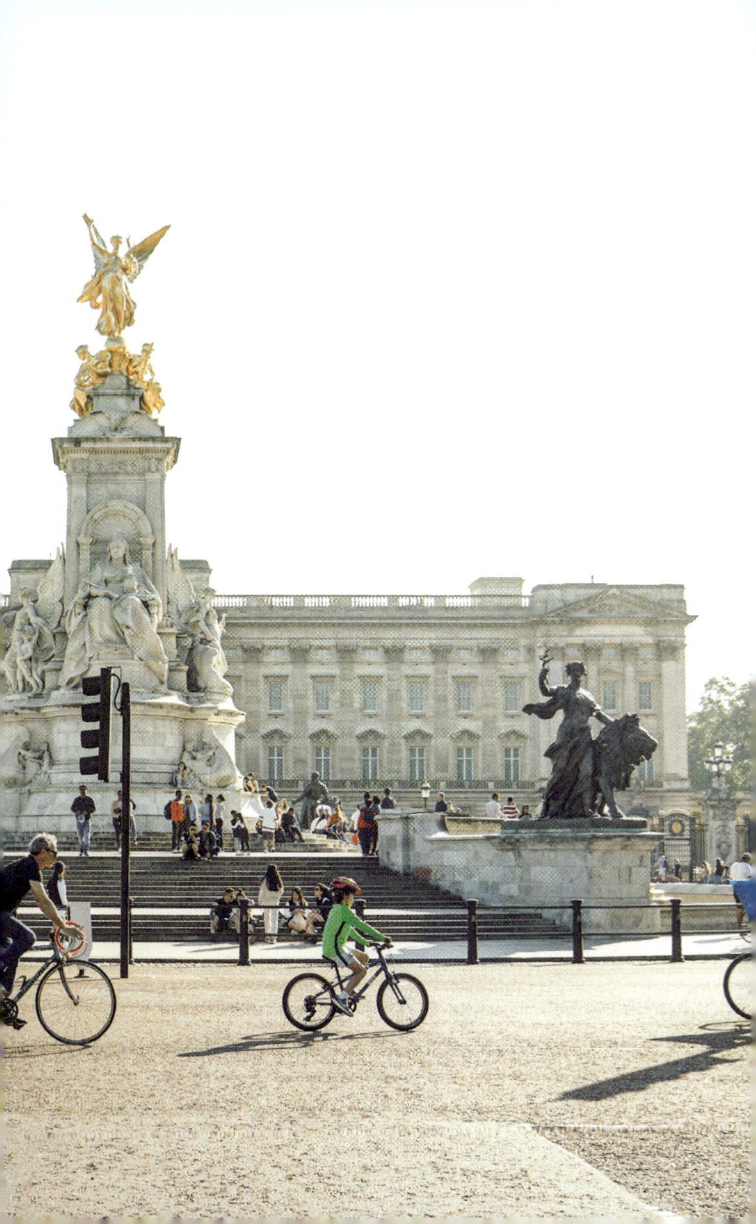

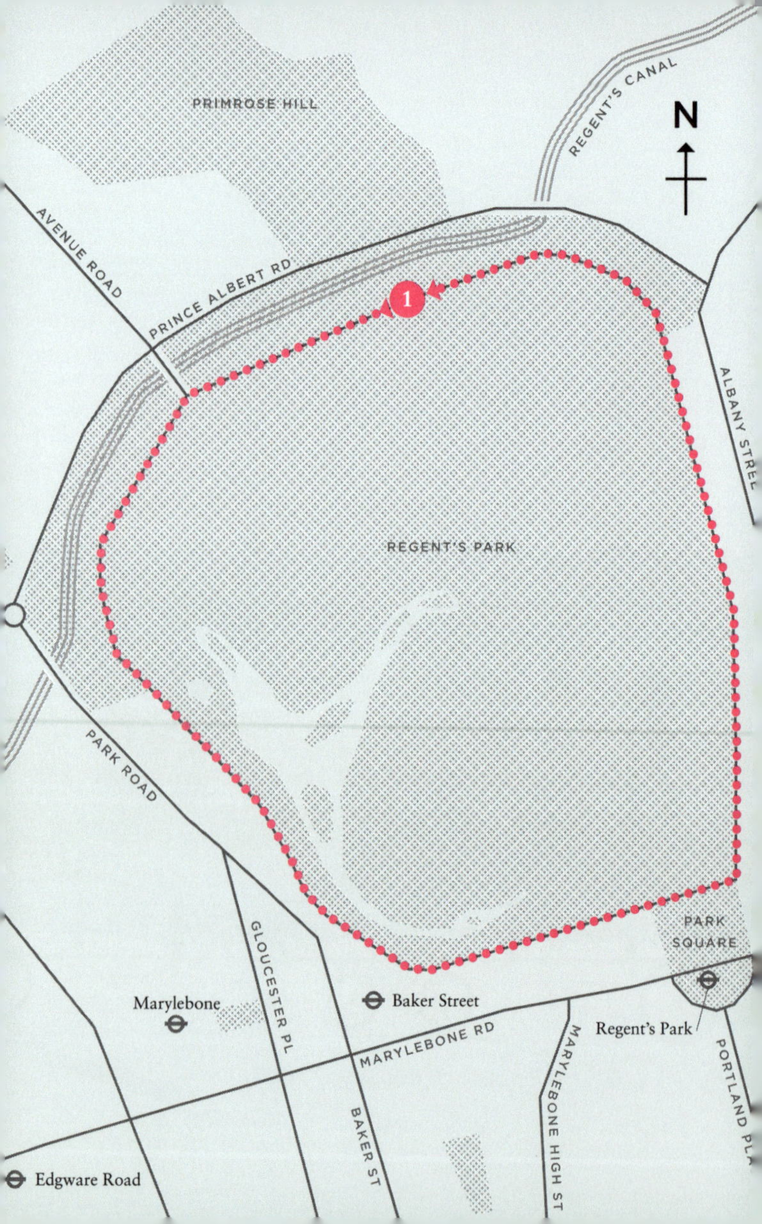

PRIMROSE HILL
REGENT'S CANAL
N
AVENUE ROAD
PRINCE ALBERT RD
1
ALBANY STREE
REGENT'S PARK
PARK ROAD
GLOUCESTER PL
PARK
SQUARE
Marylebone
Baker Street
Regent's Park
MARYLEBONE RD
MARYLEBONE HIGH ST
PORTLAND PLA
BAKER ST
Edgware Road

RIDE 2

REGENT'S PARK LAPS

Distance: 5km / 3 miles
Riding time (w/o stops): 10–20 minutes
Difficulty: Avoid rush hour, but otherwise easy

Regent's Park is where Lycra-clad gladiators come to train. When it's not rush hour, this place is a haven for cyclists, with countless clubs, groups and solo riders zooming around the 5km circuit. Whatever brings you here, whether you're training for a triathlon or simply enjoying the beautiful scenery, the most important thing is to enjoy the ride. Not all of London is this bike friendly. We recommend starting at the London Zoo ❶, a popular meeting spot for cyclists and lions, then head anti-clockwise.

To see the full route scan the QR code or go to:
hoxtonminipress.com/pages/ride2

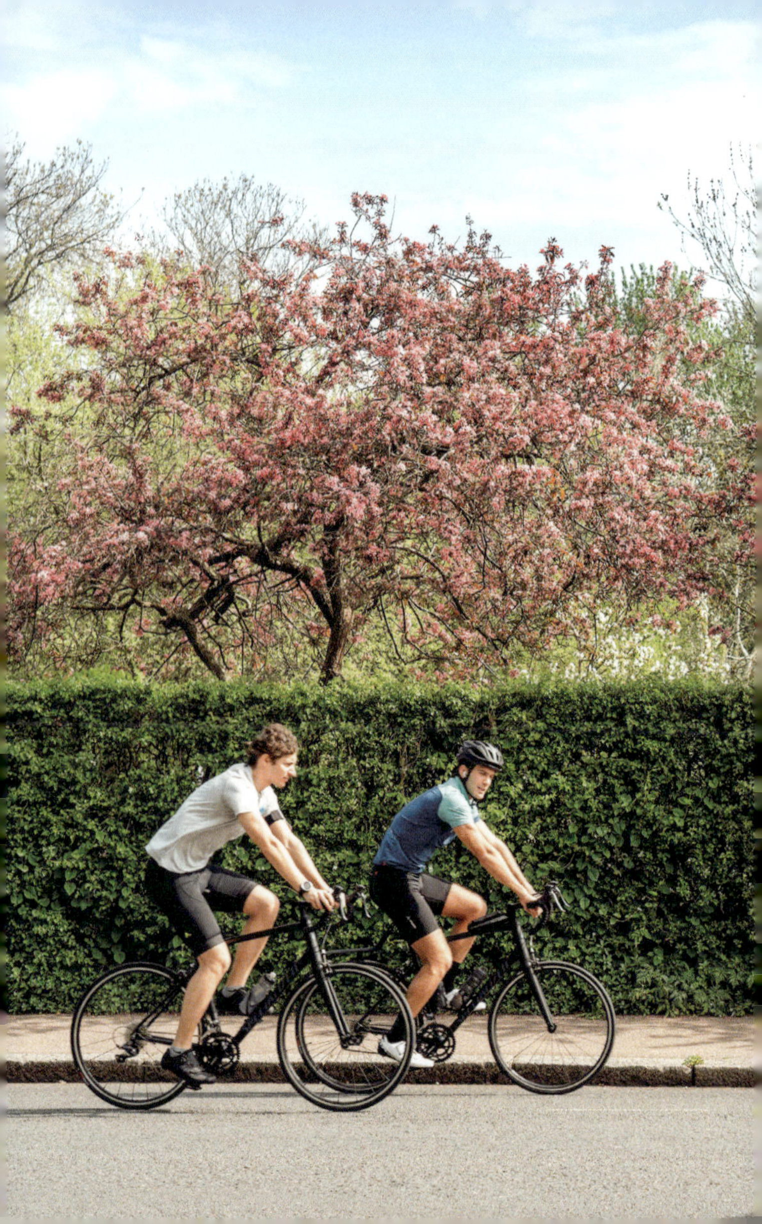

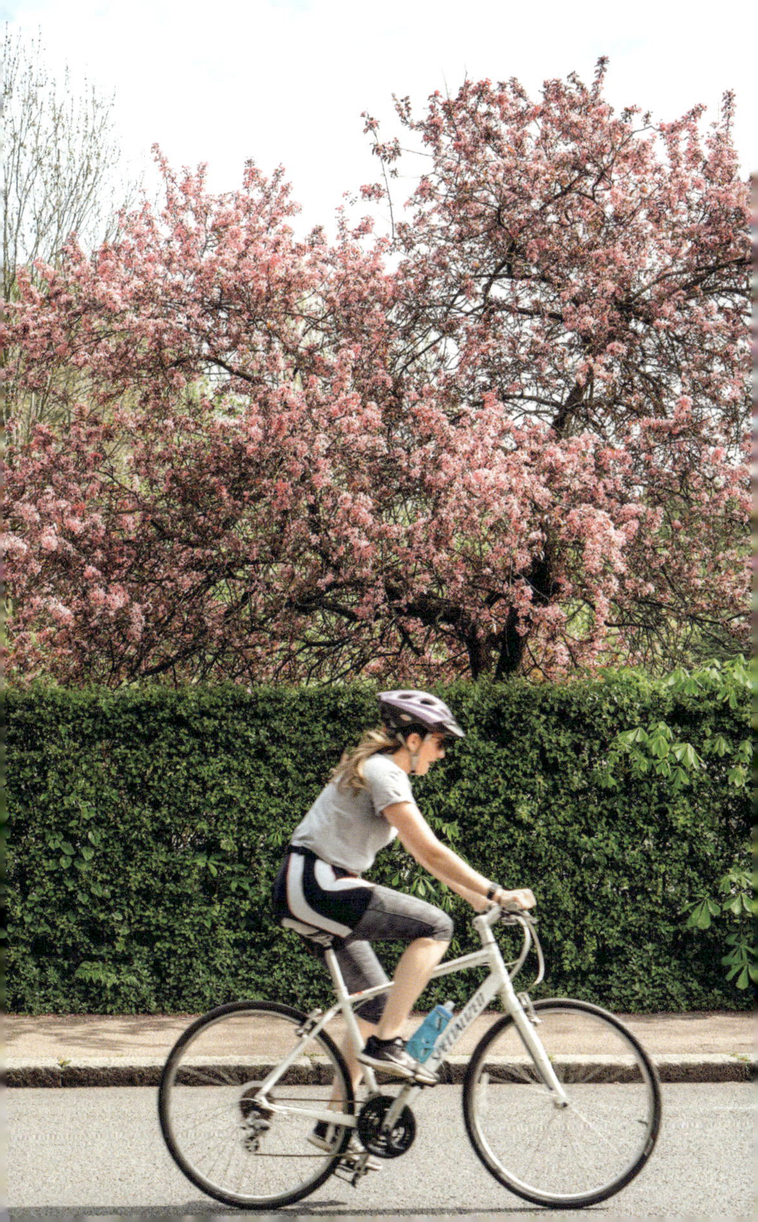

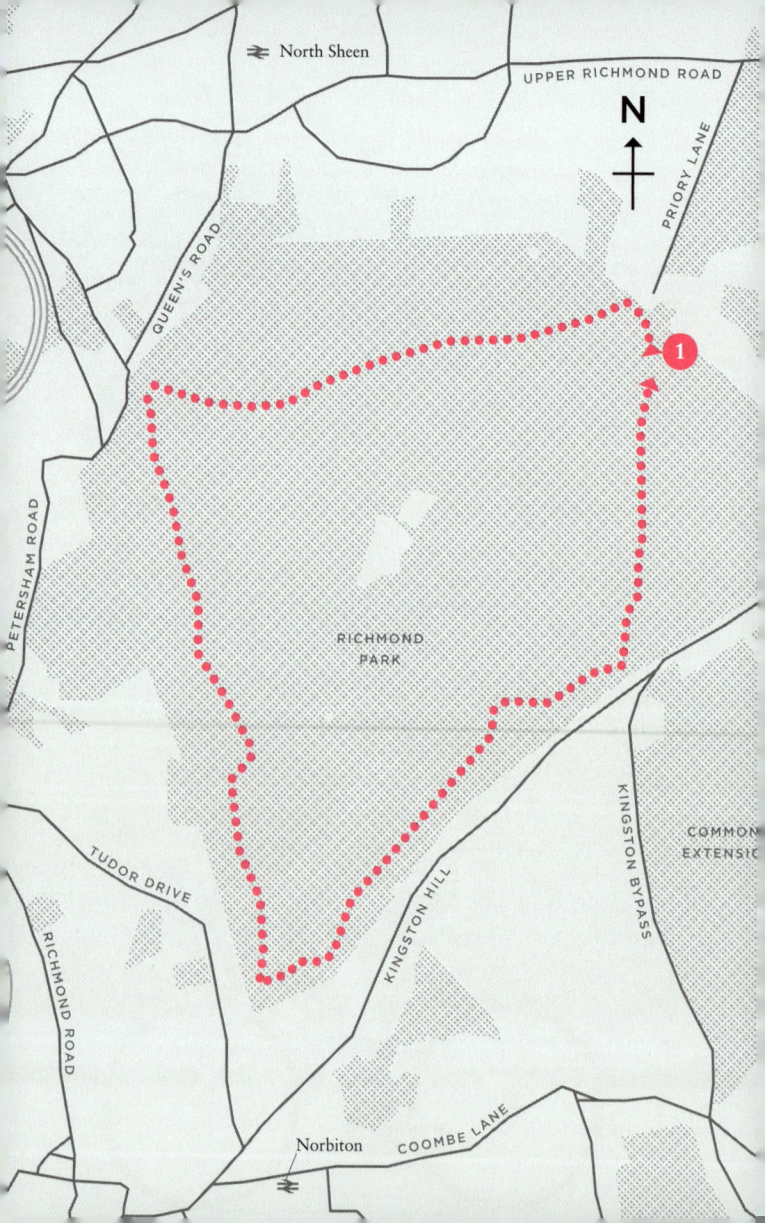

Richmond Park

- North Sheen
- UPPER RICHMOND ROAD
- PRIORY LANE
- QUEEN'S ROAD
- PETERSHAM ROAD
- RICHMOND PARK
- TUDOR DRIVE
- RICHMOND ROAD
- KINGSTON HILL
- KINGSTON BYPASS
- COMMON EXTENSION
- COOMBE LANE
- Norbiton

N

1

RIDE 3

TOUR DE RICHMOND PARK

Distance: 10km / 6 miles
Riding time (w/o stops): 25–45 minutes
Difficulty: Easy but with a few climbs

In the 17th century, when plague forced London to lockdown, King Charles I relocated his frolicking court to Richmond Park. This majestic spot still feels like an escape from the crowds. The park's 10km loop is a cult cycling destination, with sweeping views over the Thames Valley and a climb that is sure to test your thighs. Look out for wild deer that often come strangely close (introduced by the aforementioned monarch) and bright green parakeets. Start and end with a coffee at Collici's Cafe ❶ and repeat the lap as many times you like.

To see the full route scan the QR code or go to:
hoxtonminipress.com/pages/ride3

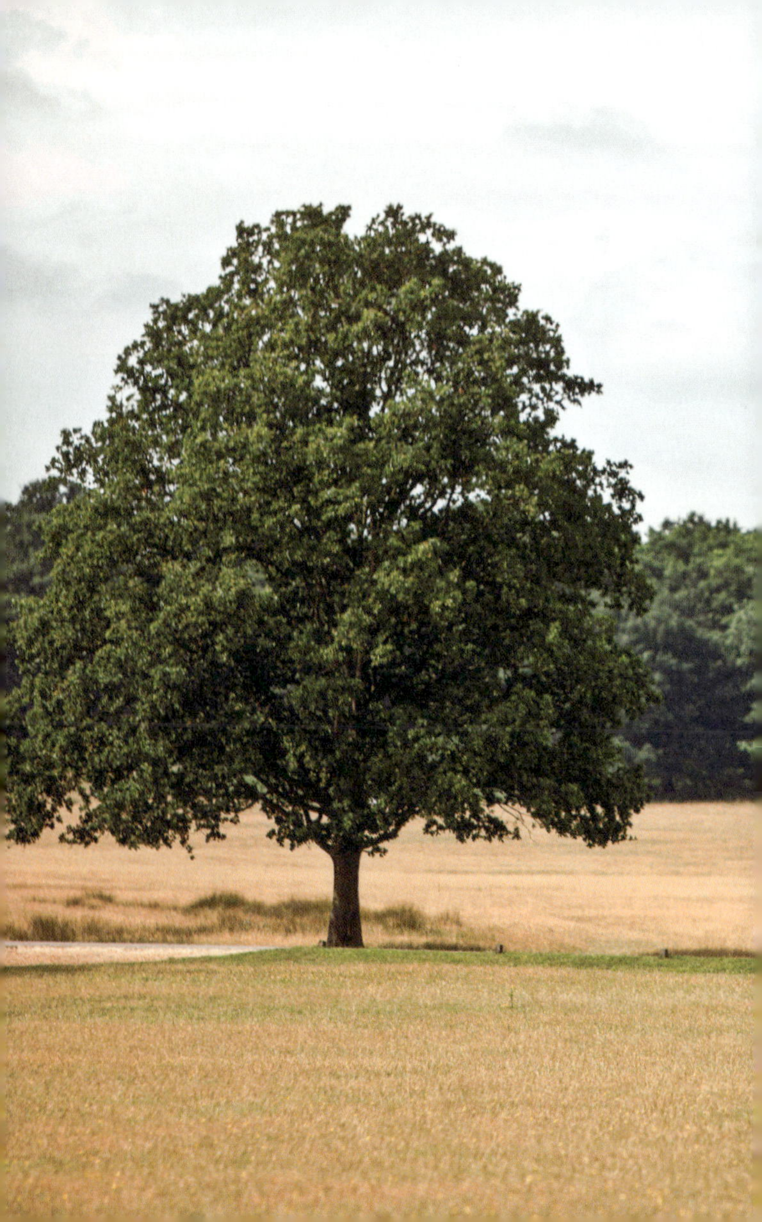

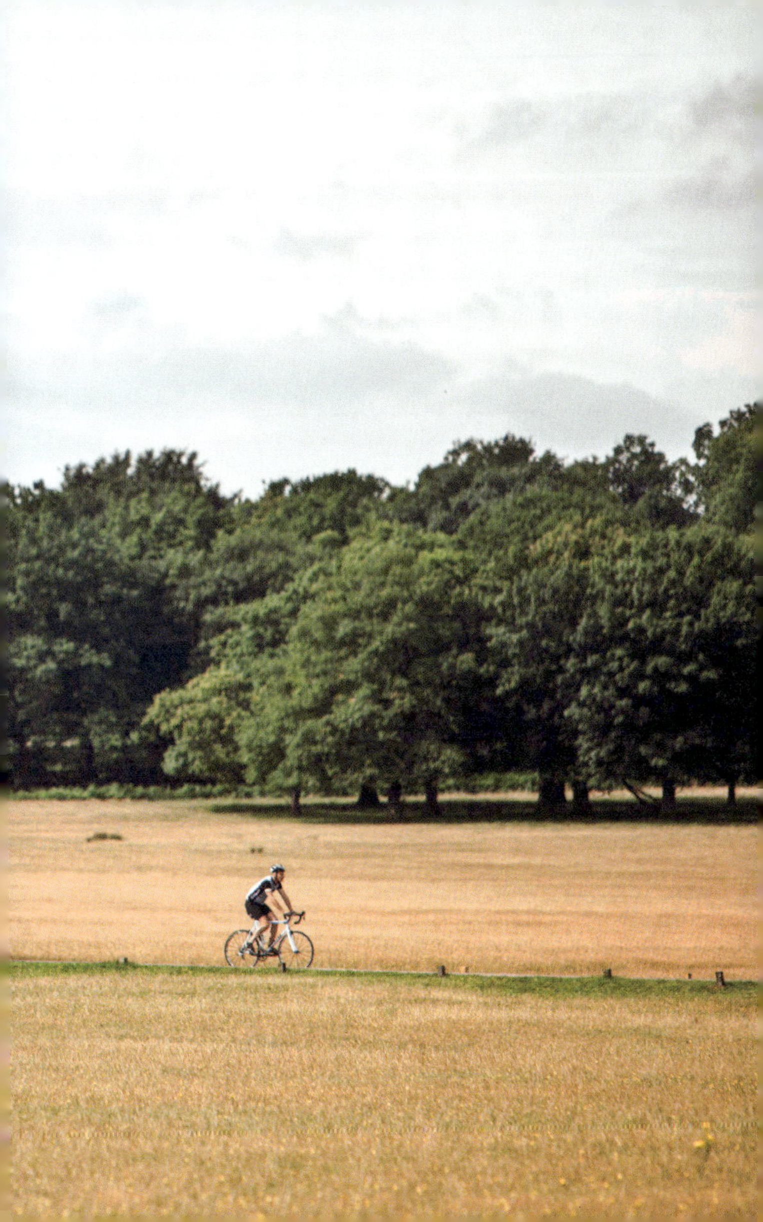

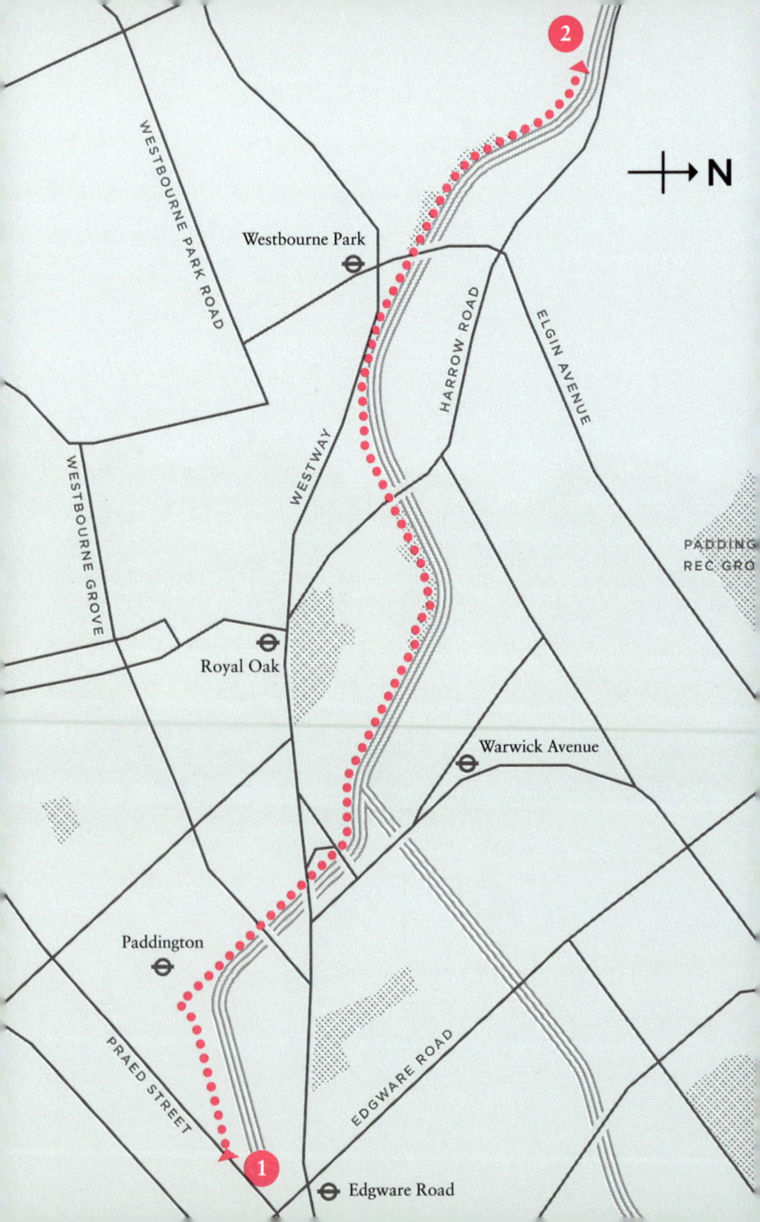
2
N
Westbourne Park
WESTBOURNE PARK ROAD
HARROW ROAD
ELGIN AVENUE
WESTWAY
WESTBOURNE GROVE
PADDING
REC GRO
Royal Oak
Warwick Avenue
Paddington
PRAED STREET
EDGWARE ROAD
1
Edgware Road

RIDE 4

GRAND UNION CANAL

Distance: 6km / 4 miles (there and back)
Riding time (w/o stops): 20–35 minutes
Difficulty: Very easy but expect pedestrians

This gentle but uplifting route starts from the Paddington Basin ❶ and follows the Grand Union Canal towpath, past colourful houseboats with flourishing veg patches. There's no traffic, aside from the odd runner, so it's the perfect jaunt for cautious cyclists. Although this canal is the longest in Britain (by boat, you can go all the way to Birmingham), we think it's worth finishing at the Canal Deli ❷ to refuel with a flat white and homemade sandwich before heading home the way you came.

To see the full route scan the QR code or go to:
hoxtonminipress.com/pages/ride4

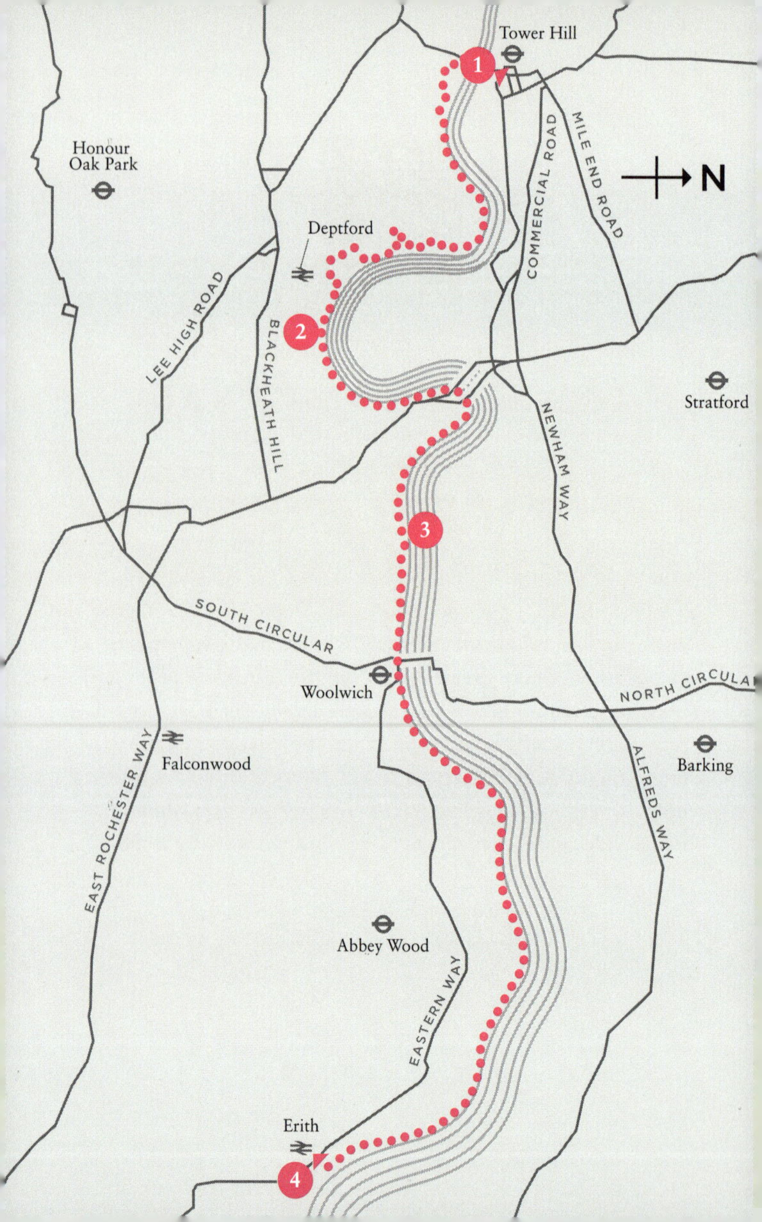
Tower Hill
1
N
Honour Oak Park
Deptford
COMMERCIAL ROAD
MILE END ROAD
LEE HIGH ROAD
2
BLACKHEATH HILL
Stratford
NEWHAM WAY
3
SOUTH CIRCULAR
Woolwich
NORTH CIRCULA
Falconwood
EAST ROCHESTER WAY
Barking
ALFREDS WAY
Abbey Wood
EASTERN WAY
Erith
4

RIDE 5

THAMES PATH, OUT EAST

Distance: 30km / 19 miles (one way)
Riding time (w/o stops): 1.5–2 hours
Difficulty: Generally easy, very flat, some pedestrians

The Thames Path, which travels alongside London's biggest river, runs all the way from Gloucester to Kent, but you can join this mostly traffic-free route at Tower Bridge ❶ and follow it through the Victorian streets of Bermondsey, passing the iconic Cutty Sark ❷ in Greenwich as you head towards the Thames Barrier ❸. Soak up some of Britain's industrial and maritime history before continuing along the riverbank until you reach Erith ❹, where you can hop on a train home or, if you're feeling fresh enough, grab an ice cream before cycling back. If you bike both ways, it's a manageable (38 miles in all) and enjoyable day trip.

To see the full route scan the QR code or go to:
hoxtonminipress.com/pages/ride5

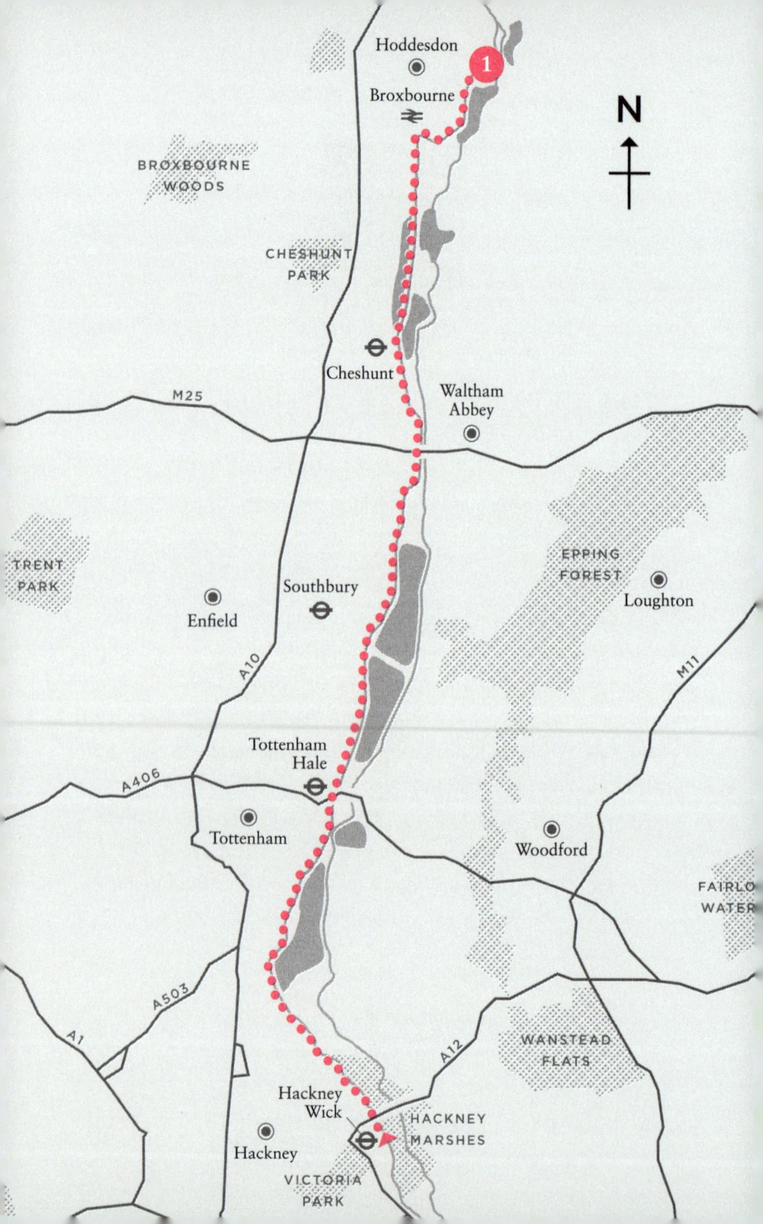

Hoddesdon
1
Broxbourne
N
BROXBOURNE
WOODS
CHESHUNT
PARK
Cheshunt
Waltham
Abbey
M25
EPPING
FOREST
Loughton
TRENT
PARK
Enfield
Southbury
A10
M11
Tottenham
Hale
A406
Tottenham
Woodford
FAIRLO
WATER
A503
A1
A12
WANSTEAD
FLATS
Hackney
Wick
HACKNEY
MARSHES
Hackney
VICTORIA
PARK

RIDE 6

UP THE LEA VALLEY

Distance: 54km / 33.5 miles (there and back)
Riding time (w/o stops): 2–3.5 hours
Difficulty: Easy but on very light gravel

This surprisingly rural route will take you out into the hinterlands of London. Hackney Wick is a great place to start, with plenty of cafes to choose from before you make for the marshes. Almost immediately, you will see a different side of the city and its surrounding countryside. You can cut the route short and come back the way you came at any point, although we recommend making it to the Fish and Eels ❶, a perfect pit stop for lunch before returning home. The route is mostly smooth gravel so should suit all bikes, just be aware that it can get very muddy after rain.

To see the full route scan the QR code or go to:
hoxtonminipress.com/pages/ride6

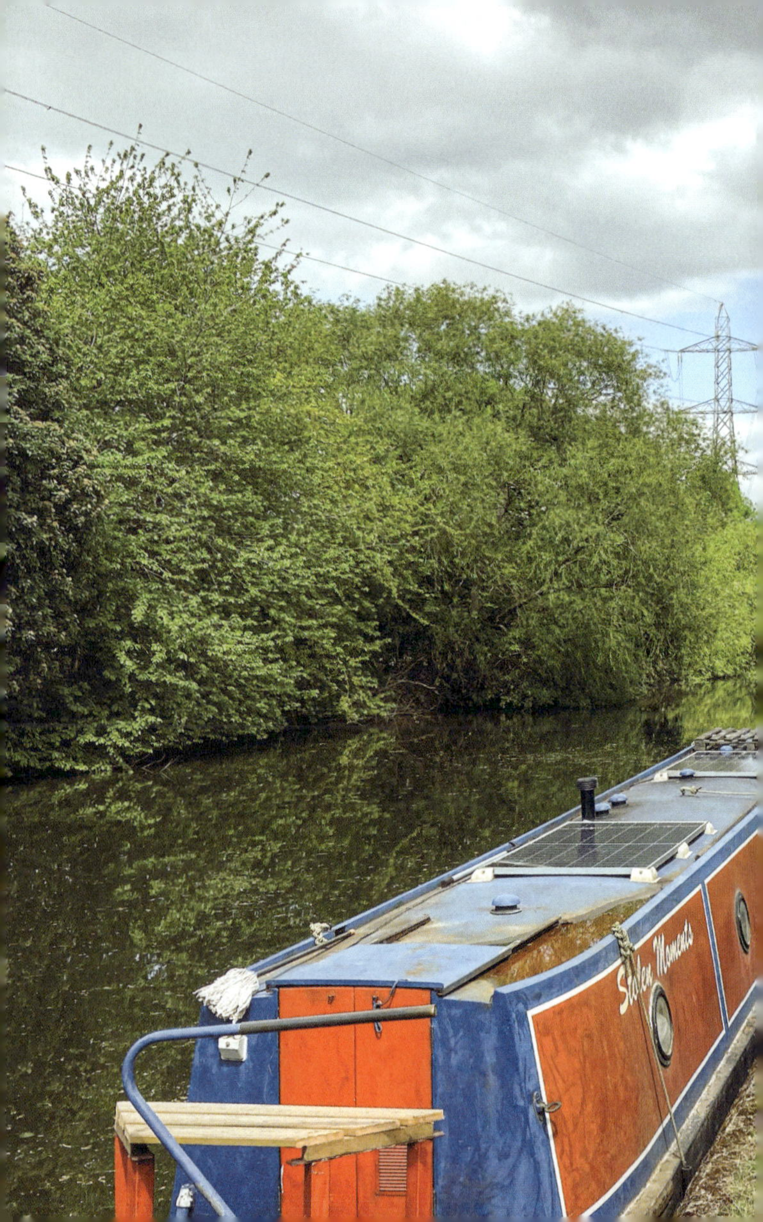
Stolen Moments

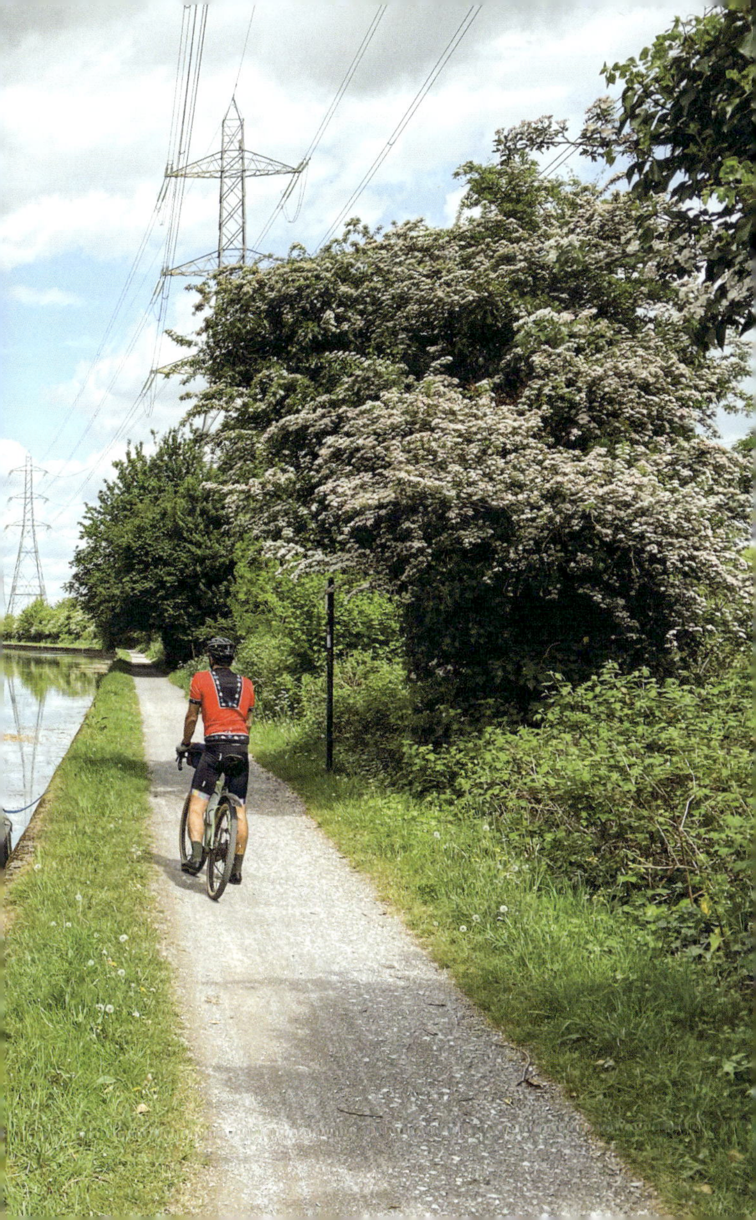

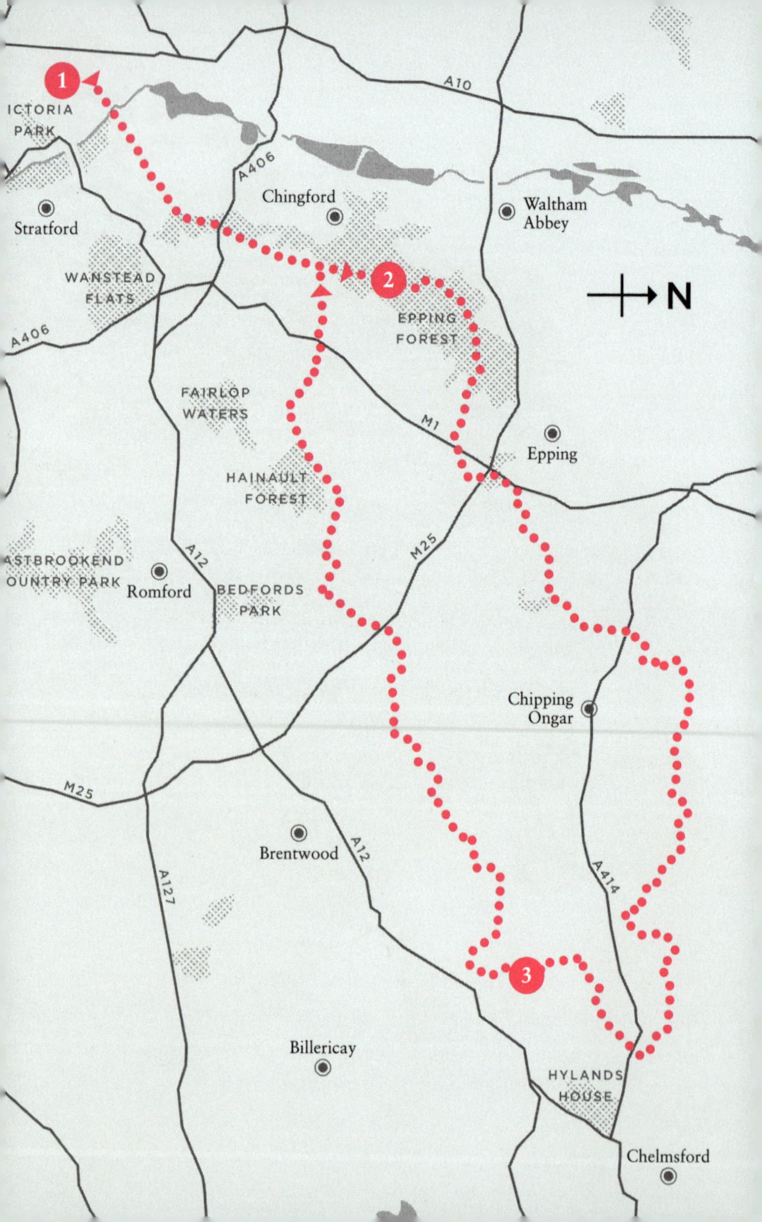
1
ICTORIA PARK
Stratford
WANSTEAD FLATS
A406
A406
Chingford
A10
Waltham Abbey
2
EPPING FOREST
N
FAIRLOP WATERS
M1
Epping
HAINAULT FOREST
ASTBROOKEND OUNTRY PARK
Romford
A12
BEDFORDS PARK
M25
Chipping Ongar
M25
Brentwood
A12
A127
A414
3
Billericay
HYLANDS HOUSE
Chelmsford

RIDE 7

BEYOND EPPING FOREST

Distance: 104km / 65 miles
Riding time (w/o stops): 4–7 hours
Difficulty: Some hills. Expect traffic while escaping town

Cycle through the ancient woodland of Epping Forest and out into the winding lanes of Essex. Start outside the dramatic Clapton Hart (conveniently it's next to Hub Vélo [no.8]) ❶, and then follow the cycle path through Walthamstow before taking the main road out into Epping Forest ❷. It is the largest forest in London and has a long, fascinating history, so take your time to explore. After that, you're in a cyclist's paradise of quiet lanes and charming villages. Fancy some lunch? The Viper at Mill Green ❸ is about halfway and serves up traditional pub grub in a cosy setting. Head back to where you started for another bite or tipple at The Clapton Hart.

To see the full route scan the QR code or go to:
hoxtonminipress.com/pages/ride7

Riding fast and slow around Epping Forest

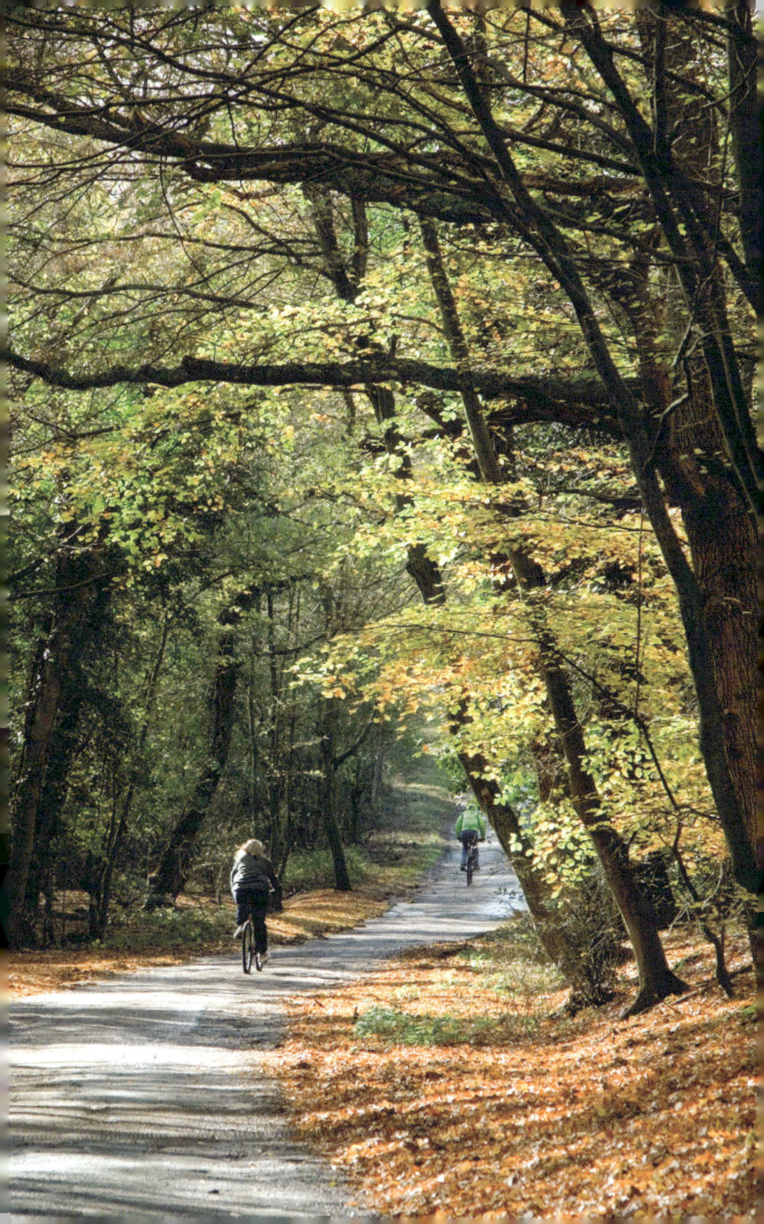

Weybridge
M25
A3
N
A243
Epsom
A24
Woking
1
Leatherhead
A3
M25
Guildford
2
Dorking
SURREY HILLS
AONB
A24
Cranleigh
A264

RIDE 8

THE SURREY HILLS

Distance: 85km / 53 miles
Riding time (w/o stops): 3.5 – 5.5 hours
Difficulty: Pleasant roads but some steep hills

This one requires you to take the train out to Cobham ❶ from Waterloo, cycling out of the station and into the bucolic surrounds of Surrey. This pastoral ride partly follows the circuit used for the 2012 Olympic road race (although they had to do nine laps, whereas we think one is more than enough). Follow undulating lanes, skirting around Dorking, before taking on the iconic Box Hill ❷ via the infamous zig-zag road. This big climb is not steep but it is long (4km). Luckily, there's a bustling cafe at the top so you can have a well-earned break, before heading downhill all the way back to the start.

To see the full route scan the QR code or go to:
hoxtonminipress.com/pages/ride8

The view from the top of Box Hill
Opposite: Up the zig-zag road to get there

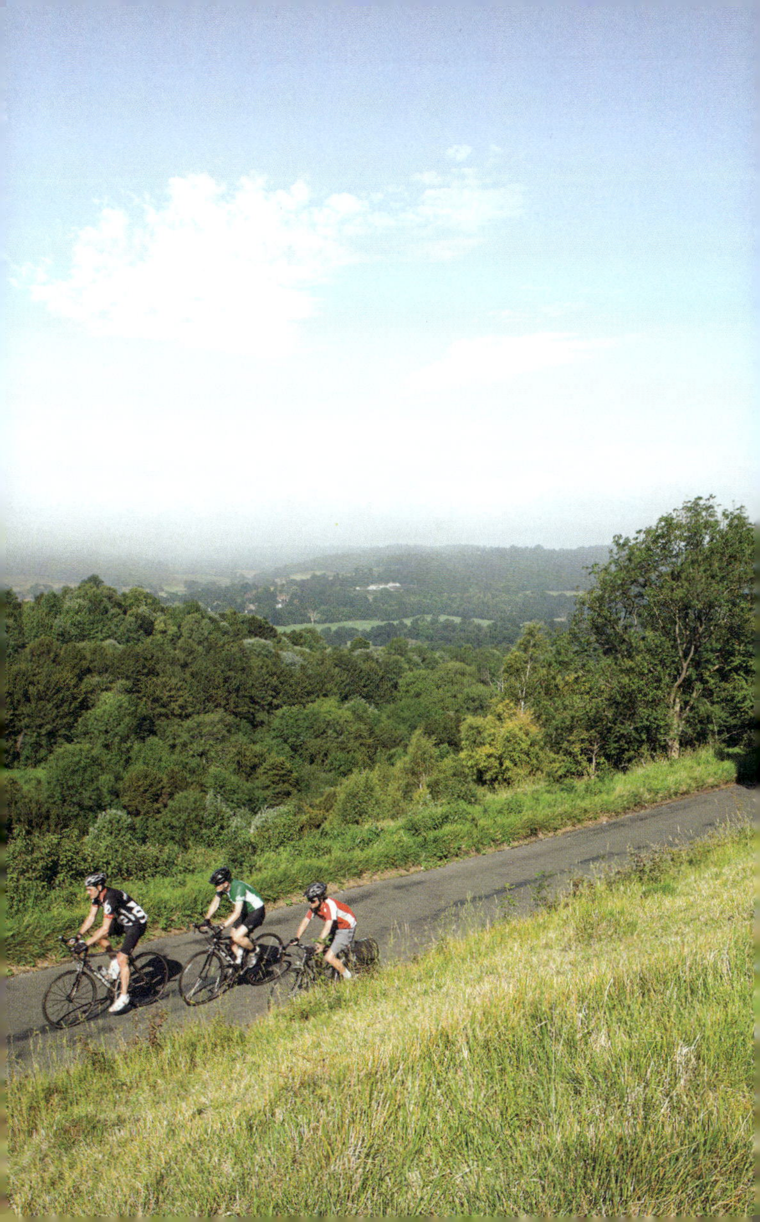

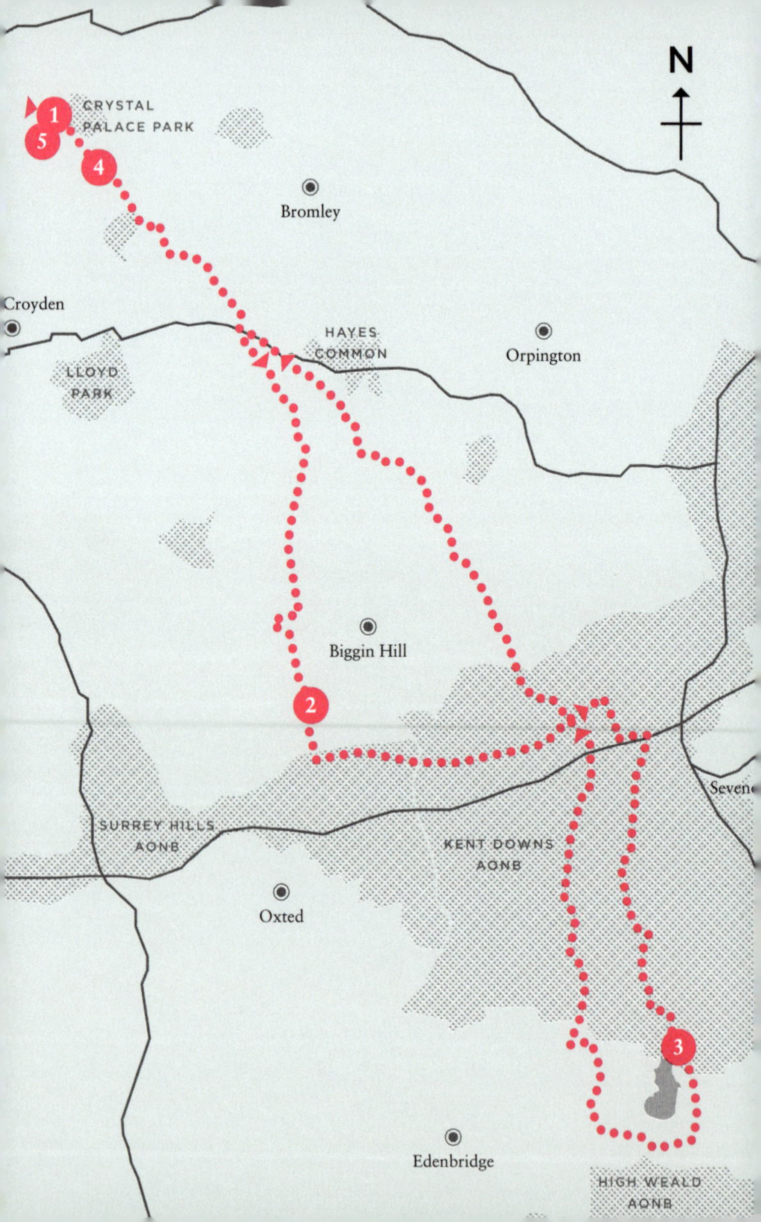
N
1
5
4
CRYSTAL
PALACE PARK
Bromley
Croyden
HAYES
COMMON
Orpington
LLOYD
PARK
Biggin Hill
2
Seven
SURREY HILLS
AONB
KENT DOWNS
AONB
Oxted
3
Edenbridge
HIGH WEALD
AONB

RIDE 9

THE KENT HILLS

Distance: 75km / 47 miles
Riding time (w/o stops): 3–5 hours
Difficulty: A hard ride, some very steep hills

This route is a leg buster, covering Kent's biggest climbs including the infamously steep Toy's Hill. Start at Crystal Palace ❶ and, within minutes, you'll be zipping along rambling country lanes. At the top of Beddlestead ❷ the view opens out to reveal why Kent is called the Garden of England. There are some other awe-inspiring sights, including the ancient Pilgrims Way and Bough Beech Reservoir ❸. Remember to reserve energy for Anerley ❹, the final climb – if it doesn't finish you off, then glide (mostly) downhill to legendary cycling cafe Four Boroughs ❺, the ideal place to put your feet up and swap horror stories.

To see the full route scan the QR code or go to:
hoxtonminipress.com/pages/ride9

Ide Hill down to the Bough Beech Reservoir
Opposite: The Pilgrims Way

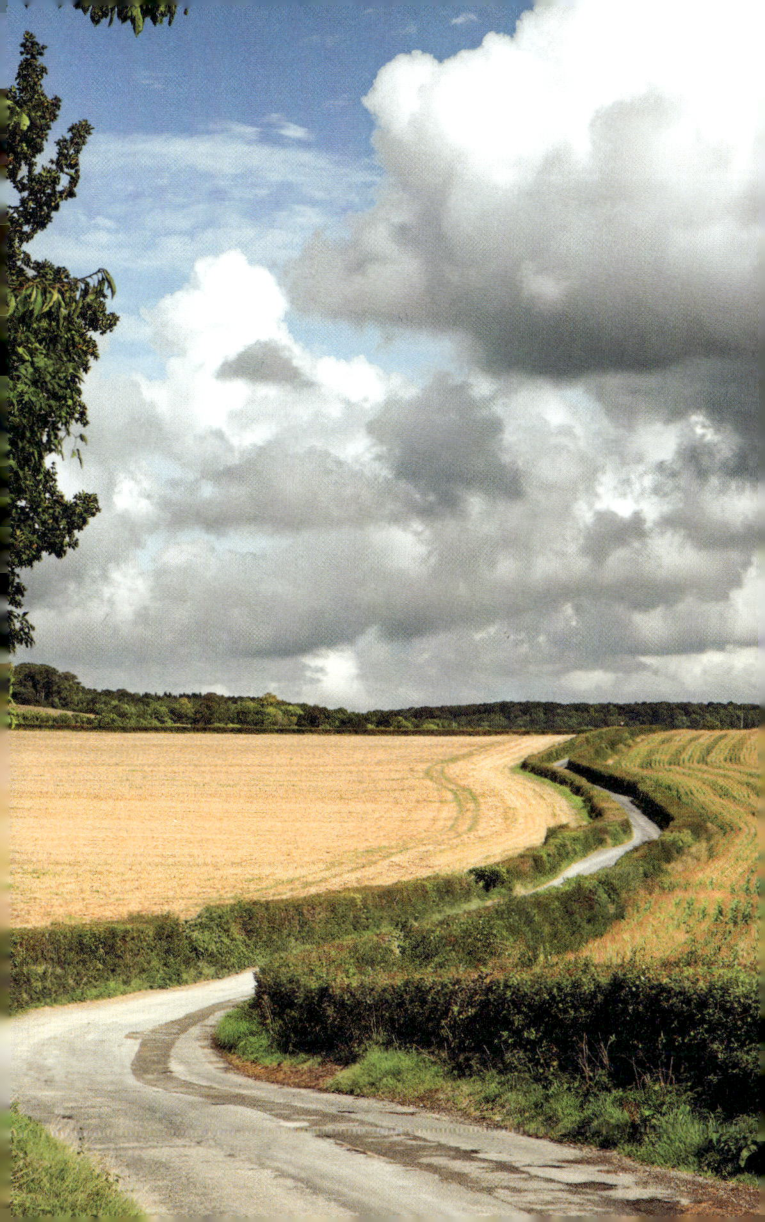

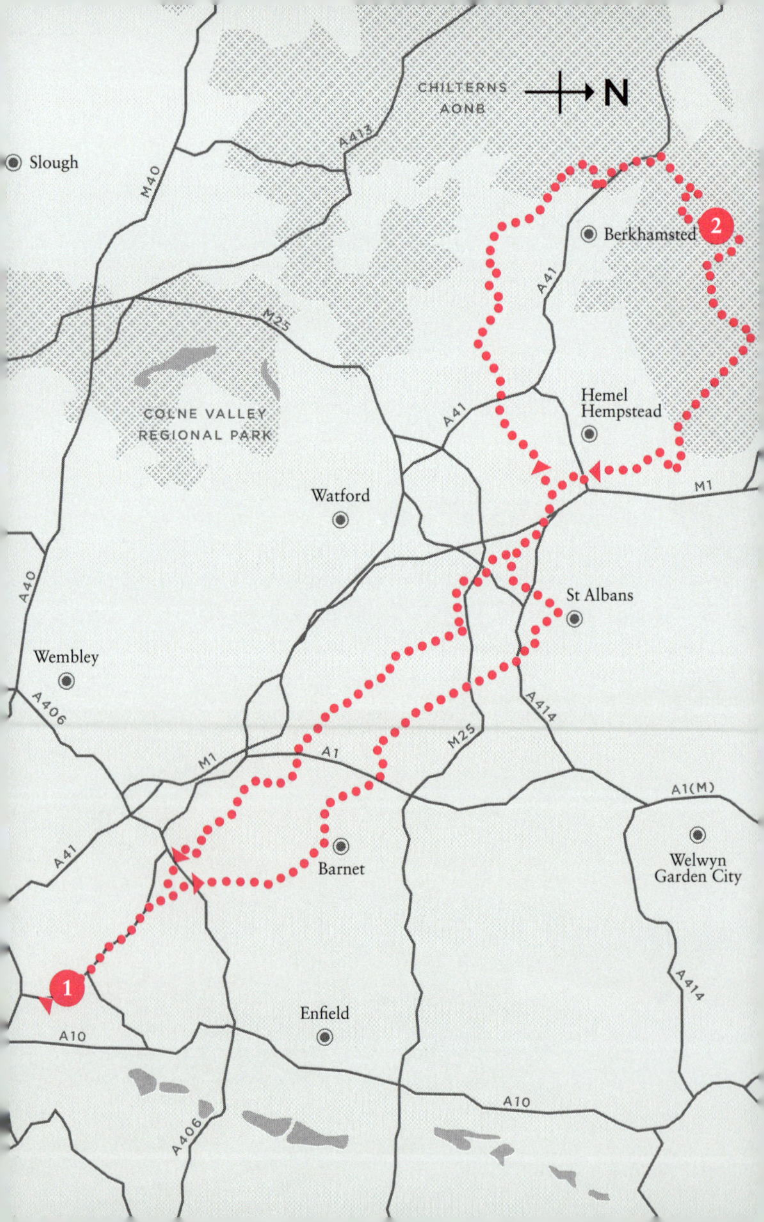
CHILTERNS AONB
N
Slough
M40
A413
Berkhamsted
A41
M25
COLNE VALLEY REGIONAL PARK
Hemel Hempstead
A41
M1
Watford
A40
St Albans
Wembley
A406
A414
M25
A1
M1
A1(M)
Welwyn Garden City
A41
Barnet
1
2
Enfield
A10
A414
A10
A406

RIDE 10

ESCAPE TO THE CHILTERNS

Distance: 128km / 79.5 miles
Riding time (w/o stops): 5–8.5 hours
Terrain: Good roads but with a lot of climbing

A big day out for cyclists who need a break from the city, this is quite a long ride so you will want to leave in the morning and give yourself plenty of time for breaks, but it is definitely worth it. Begin with a substantial breakfast in Highbury & Islington ❶ before fleeing the city for greener lands. The lanes around the Chiltern Hills are some of the quietest and most atmospheric within reach of London. The Bridgewater Arms ❷ is a great lunch spot about halfway along the route – plus, it comes just after the hardest climb. Help yourself to a hearty portion of sausages and mash before a leisurely cycle home past fields and wooded lanes.

To see the full route scan the QR code or go to:
hoxtonminipress.com/pages/ride10

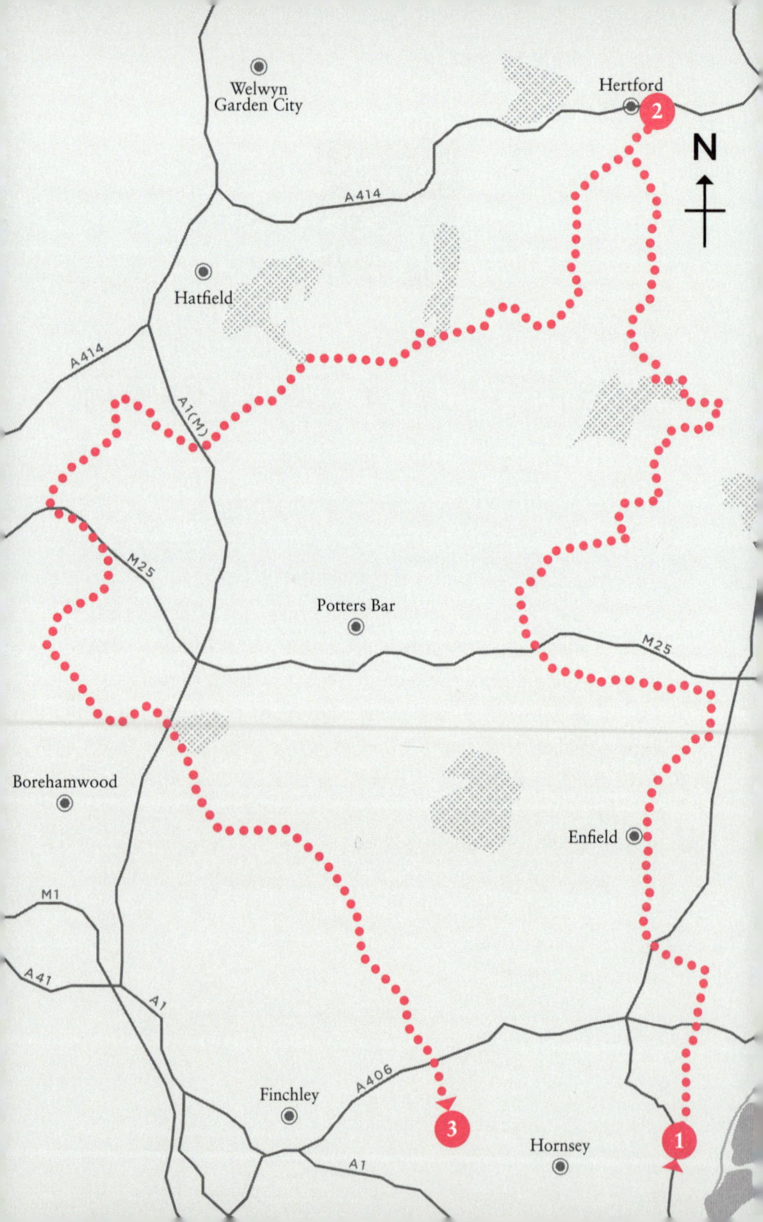

Welwyn Garden City
Hertford
2
N
A414
Hatfield
A414
A1(M)
M25
Potters Bar
M25
Borehamwood
Enfield
M1
A41
A1
A406
Finchley
3
Hornsey
1
A1

RIDE 11

WINDING LANES OF HERTFORDSHIRE

Distance: 79km / 49 miles
Riding time (w/o stops): 3–5.5 hours
Difficulty: pleasant but with short, punchy hills

There's no pretty way out of the city from north London, but this route starting in Tottenham Hale ❶ is the quickest, so you can at least make a swift escape into the hills of Hertfordshire. There are a number of short, sharp climbs that will test your stamina, but the hedgerow-lined lanes are idyllic, so take your time. Stop off in the pretty market town of Hertford ❷, where you can order an enlivening espresso at the excellent Hertford Coffee Lab. From there, make your way to Muswell Hill ❸ where plenty of pubs await thirsty cyclists.

To see the full route scan the QR code or go to:
hoxtonminipress.com/pages/ride11

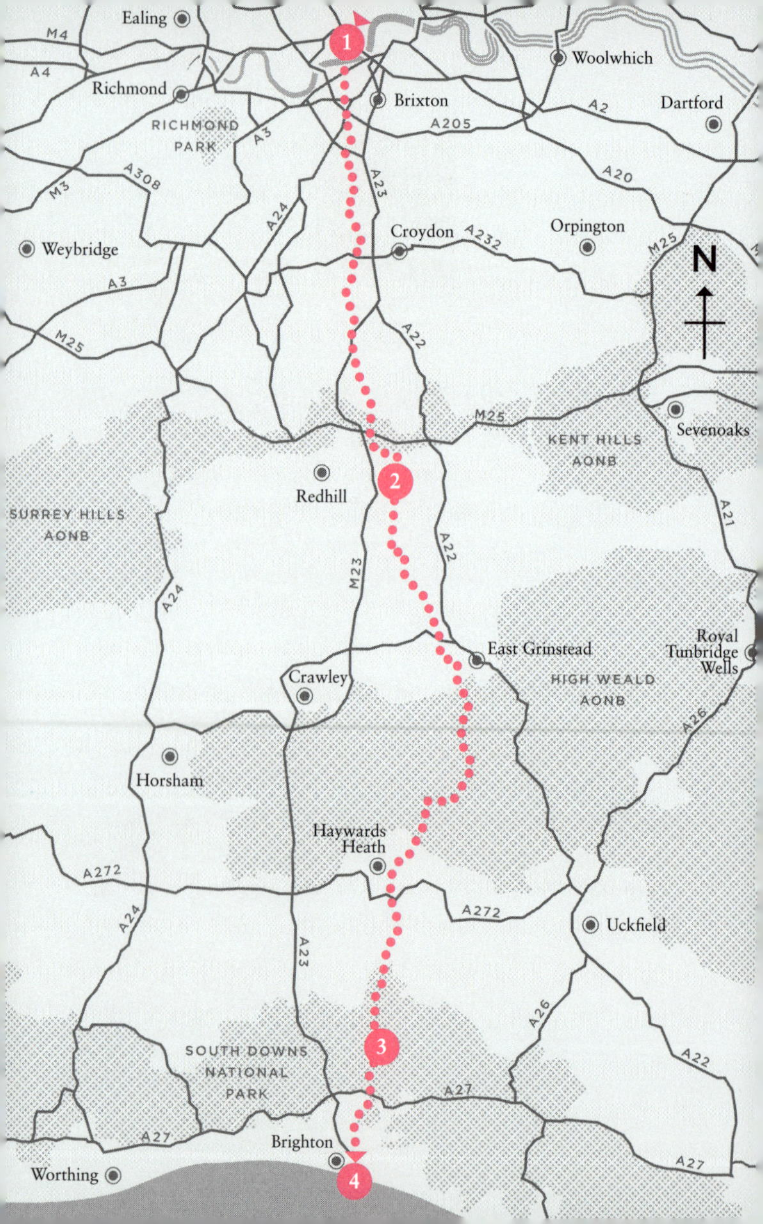

Ealing
M4
A4
Richmond
RICHMOND PARK
A3
A308
M3
Weybridge
A24
A3
M25
Brixton
A205
A23
Woolwhich
A2
Dartford
A20
Croydon
A232
Orpington
M25
N
A22
M25
KENT HILLS AONB
Sevenoaks
Redhill
SURREY HILLS AONB
M23
A22
A21
A24
East Grinstead
Royal Tunbridge Wells
HIGH WEALD AONB
Crawley
A26
Horsham
Haywards Heath
A272
A272
A24
Uckfield
A23
A26
SOUTH DOWNS NATIONAL PARK
A22
A27
A27
Brighton
A27
Worthing
1
2
3
4

RIDE 12

THE ULTIMATE LONDON-BRIGHTON

Distance: 95km / 59 miles (one way)
Riding time (w/o stops): 4–6.5 hours
Difficulty: Very manageable but with one big climb at end

Every June, cyclists gather to join the British Heart Foundation's charity ride from London to Brighton. But if you want to do it year-round, we recommend this route which starts in St James's Park ❶ and avoids the main roads so you can enjoy the surrounding countryside. Stop in Bletchingley (Lamingtons teahouse ❷ has a dreamy array of cakes) before tackling the unforgettable Ditchling Beacon ❸ climb. It's not the steepest hill, but it is long, and there are some tight corners. Have a rest at the top, taking in glorious views over the South Downs, before moseying downhill for fish and chips and/or a pint on the beach ❹.

To see the full route scan the QR code or go to:
hoxtonminipress.com/pages/ride12

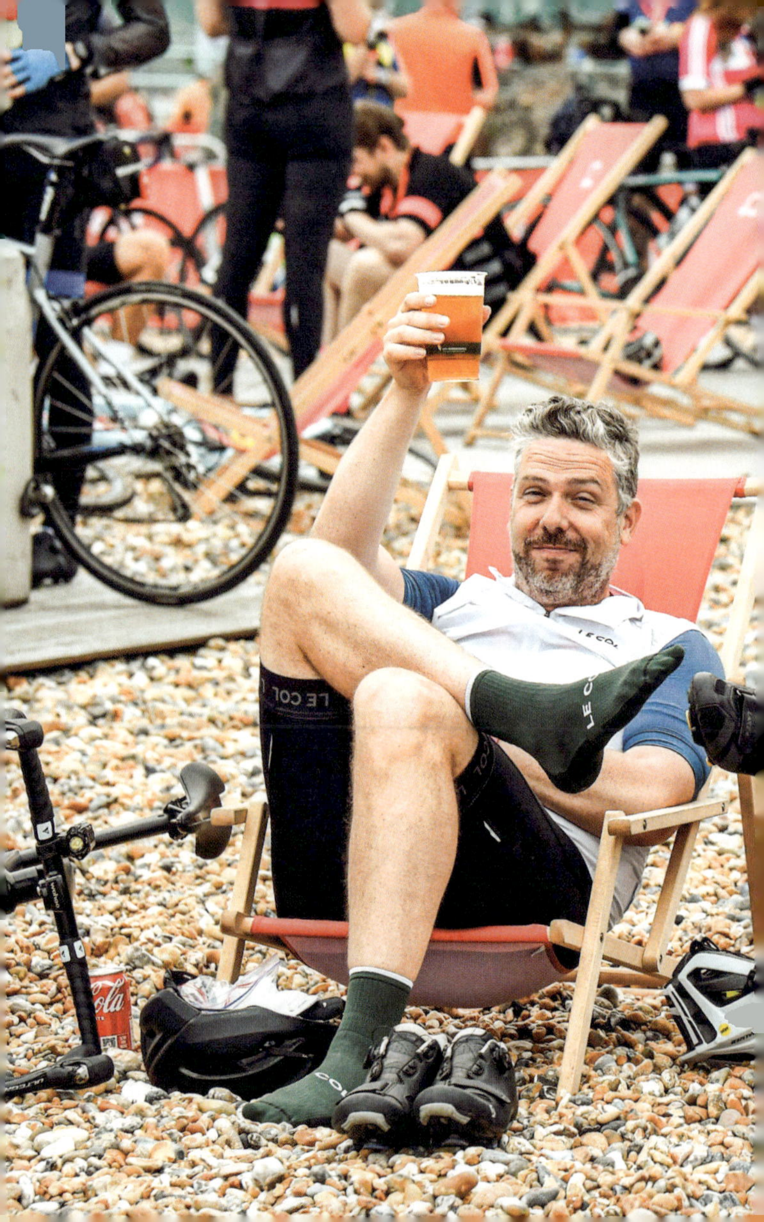
LE COL

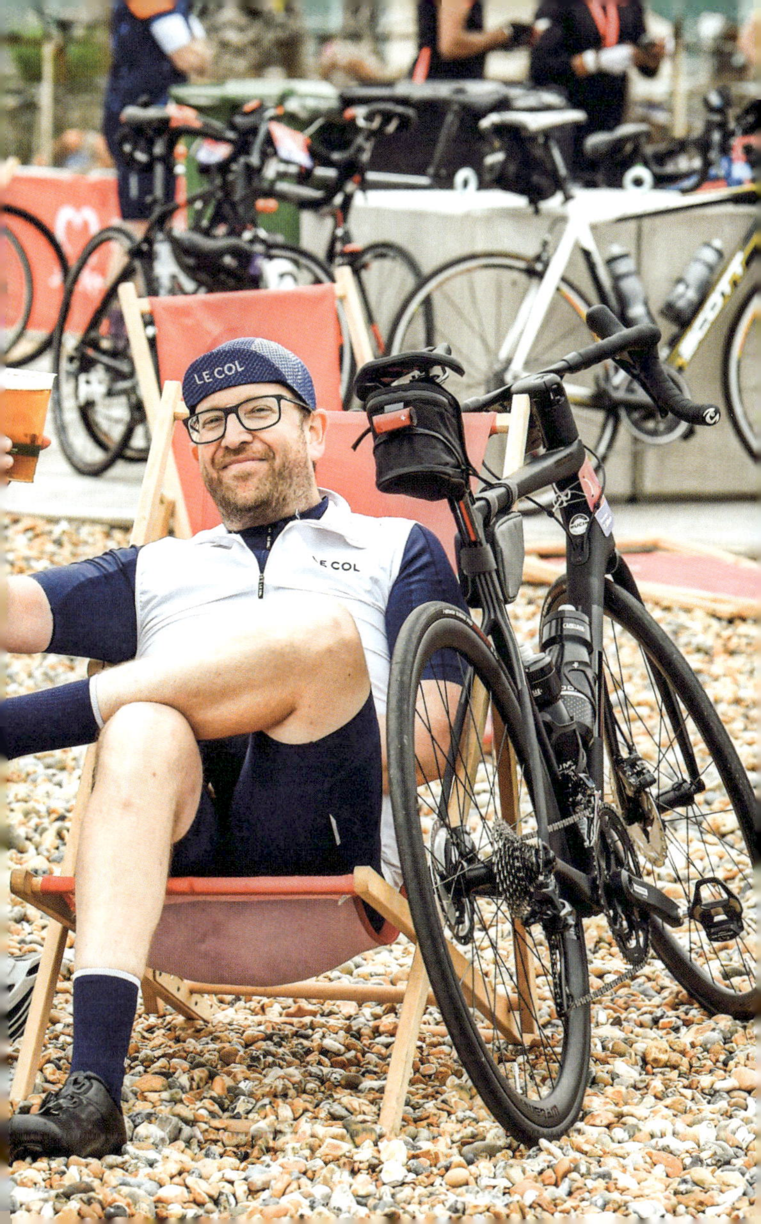
LE COL
LE COL

IMAGE CREDITS

Temple Cycles (p.4) ©Rebecca Hope; cyclists (p.5) ©Becky Marshall; cyclist in Richmond Park (p.6) ©Sung Kuk Kim / Alamy Stock Photo; cyclist on Victoria Embankment (p.7) ©James Hadley / Alamy Stock Photo; Epping Forest (p.8) ©Martin Usborne; Via Atelier (p.9) ©Martin Usborne; Condor Cycles (all images) ©Charlotte Schreiber; tokyobike (all images) ©Charlotte Schreiber; CycleFit (all images), courtesy of CycleFit; Pedal Me ©Becky Bryant – Becky Takes Photos, images from the wedding of Charlotte and Joshua Morgan; London Cycling Campaign ©Chun Chiu, courtesy of the London Cycling Campaign; Brompton Bike Hire, by George Marshall courtesy of Brompton; OurBike ©Charlotte Schreiber; Hub Vélo (all images) ©Andy Donohoe; Stayer (first image) ©Simon Weller; (second image) ©Ev Sekkides; Temple Cycles (first image) ©Rebecca Hope; (second and third images) ©Matt Mears; Dunwich Dynamo (first image) ©Martin Usborne; (second image) ©Adam Bowie; Lee Valley VeloPark (first image) ©Michael Preston / Alamy Stock Photo; (second image) ©Marcin Rogozinski / Alamy Stock Photo; Black Uniter Bike Ride (all images) ©Simon Robers; Freddie Grubb (first image) ©Freddie Grubb; (second image) ©Amelia Rae Perry; (third image) ©Pepijn Tyvaert; Quirk Cycles (all images) ©Nikoo Hamzavi; Burgess Park BMX Track (all images) ©Samuel Hicks; The Bike Project ©Charlotte Schreiber; NipNip (all images) ©Charlotte Schreiber; The Dynamo (all images) ©Charlotte Schreiber; Herne Hill Velodrome ©Adam Scott; Brixton Cycles ©Becky Marshall; Gloria (all images) ©John Gordon / ZF Media; XO ©Charlotte Schreiber; Pearson ©The Times / News Licensing; Fully Charges ©Charlotte Schreiber; Seabass Cycles ©Charlotte Schreiber; Rapha London Clubhouse (all images) ©Charlotte Schreiber; Sigma Sports, by Jake Armstrong / Sigma Sports; Pedal Back Cycling (all images) ©Nicky Redford; Fairlight Cycles (all images), by Jim Holland, images courtesy of Fairlight Cycles and Brooks; The Hackney Peddler, images courtesy of The Hackney Peddler; VIA (first image) ©Nick Frendo, courtesy of VIA; (all other images) ©Martin Usborne; Paul Smith, courtesy of Paul Smith; London Green Cycles ©Charlotte Schreiber; The Spoke (all images) ©Charlotte Schreiber; Urban Hill Climb ©Adrian Wells; Ride 1 ©Lesley Lau; Ride 2 © ilpo musto / Alamy Stock Photo; Ride 3 ©Buzz Pictures / Alamy Stock Photo; Ride 6 ©Martin Usborne; Ride 7 (first image) ©Richard Lincoln / Alamy Stock Photo; Ride 7 (second image) ©Andrew Bailey / Alamy Stock Photo; Ride 8 (first image) ©Martin Usborne; Ride 8 (second image) ©robertharding / Alamy Stock Photo; Ride 9 ©Liliya Sayfeeva / Alamy Stock Photo; Ride 9 (second image) ©Tony Watson / Alamy Stock Photo; Ride 12 ©Simon Dack News / Alamy Stock Photo.

CONTRIBUTORS

Rachel Segal Hamilton learned to pedal as a child in Cambridge, a town where you emerge from the womb on two wheels. She started commuting in London by bike in her 20s, and these days, her ride is piled high with schoolbags and children. A writer and editor, she splits her time between London and Birmingham, where she campaigns for safer cycling with *Better Streets for Birmingham*.

Hoxton Mini Press is a small indie publisher based in east London. We make books about London (and beyond) with a dedication to lovely, sustainable production and brilliant photography. When we started the company, people told us 'print was dead'; we wanted to prove them wrong. Books are no longer about information but objects in their own right: things to collect and own and inspire. We are an environmentally conscious publisher, committed to offsetting our carbon footprint. This book, for instance, is 100 per cent carbon compensated, with offset purchased from Stand for Trees.

INDEX

The Bike Project, *17*
Black Unity Bike Ride, *13*
Brixton Cycles, *21*
Brompton Bike Hire, *6*
Burgess Park BMX Track, *16*
Condor Cycles, *1*
CycleFit, *3*
Dunwich Dynamo, *11*
The Dynamo, *19*
Fairlight Cycles, *30*
Freddie Grubb, *14*
Fully Charged, *25*
Gloria, *22*
The Hackney Peddler, *31*
Herne Hill Velodrome, *20*
Hub Vélo, *8*
Lee Valley VeloPark, *12*
London Cycling Campaign, *5*

London Green Cycles, *34*
NipNip, *18*
OurBike, *7*
Paul Smith, *33*
Pearson, *24*
Pedal Back Cycling, *29*
Pedal Me, *4*
Quirk Cycles, *15*
Rapha London Clubhouse, *27*
Seabass Cycles, *26*
Sigma Sports, *28*
The Spoke, *35*
Stayer, *9*
Temple Cycles, *10*
tokyobike, *2*
Urban Hill Climb, *36*
VIA Atelier, *32*
XO Bikes, *23*

An Opinionated Guide to Cycle London
First edition, first printing

Published in 2023 by Hoxton Mini Press, London
Copyright © Hoxton Mini Press 2023. All rights reserved.

Text by Rachel Segal Hamilton
Copy-editing by Felicity Maunder
Additional design by Richard Mason
Production and editorial support by Megan Baffoe

With thanks to Matthew Young for initial series design.

Please note: we recommend checking the websites listed for each
entry before you visit for the latest information on price, opening times
and pre-booking requirements.

The right of Rachel Segal Hamilton to be identified as the creator of this Work
has been asserted under the Copyright, Designs and Patents Act 1988.

No part of this publication may be reproduced, stored in a retrieval system,
or transmitted in any form or by any means, electronic, mechanical,
photocopying, recording or otherwise, without the prior written permission
of the copyright owner.

A CIP catalogue record for this book is available from the British Library.

ISBN: 978-1-914314-50-6

Printed and bound by OZGraf, Poland

Hoxton Mini Press is an environmentally conscious publisher, committed
to offsetting our carbon footprint. This book is 100 per cent carbon
compensated, with offset purchased from Stand For Trees.

For every book you buy from our website, we plant a tree:
www.hoxtonminipress.com